GLOBAL AFRICAN PRESENCE

GLOBAL AFRICAN PRESENCE

BY

EDWARD SCOBIE

INTRODUCTION
BY
DR. IVAN VAN SERTIMA

EWORLD INC.

Buffalo, New York
14209
eeworldinc@yahoo.com

COVER DESIGN: *EWorld Inc.*
COVER ILLUSTRATION: *Andre Harris*

Library of Congress Cataloging-in-Publication Data

Scobie, Edward, 1918-1996
Global African Presence/Edward Scobie.
   p.   cm.
   Includes bibliographical references and index.
   ISBN 978-1-61759-009-2
   1. African Diaspora 2. Pan-Africanism 3. Africa—Civilization.
   4. Black Race identity. 5. Afrocentrism.I.Title.

DT16.5 .S381994   94-30327
909' .0496--dc20   CIP

Formally Published by
A&B Publishers Group
Brooklyn, New York
ISBN 1-881316-72-6

Published by

EWORLD INC.

Buffalo, New York
14209
eeworldinc@yahoo.com

11 12 13 14   6 5 4 3 2 1
Manufactured and Printed in the United States

DEDICATION

To Queen Mother Moore

*With respect, admiration and love
for your dauntless courage and steadfastness in
devoting your life to Liberation, Reparations and
Empowerment of African peoples...*

Acknowledgements

I wish to acknowledge and give sincere thanks to the sisters and brothers who helped in sundry ways to pilot this book into print.

First and foremost is Sister Norma Banks. She took the manuscript in its longhand state to her computer, and with her technical excellence, devotion, patience and love, she put everything in place and made of the finished product a work of quality. Time and monetary remuneration were absolutely of no consideration to her. Words cannot adequately describe how much love, gratitude and respect I hold for her and her family. Thank you again, Sister Norma.

I cannot forget two other sisters who also worked on the manuscript: Lori Sharpe, whose eye never misses the hidden errors which hibernate in the most professional manuscripts; and Monica, of A & B Books, who finally put everything in ship-shape order.

Encouragement, help in innumerable ways, and solid advice were always available from four dear friends whose friendship has meant everything in the world to me: Mr. J. R. Ralph Casimir, Professor Jan Carew, Dr. Ivan Van Sertima and Dr. Leonard Jeffries, Jr. The faculty and staff of the Black Studies Department at City College have been like members of a family. I cherish those twenty-one years with them. No matter what may be said by detractors, those were productive years. I meet former students all the time who testify to that fact.

Queen Mother Kefa Nephthys, Brother Bill Jones and other members of the First World Alliance have played important roles in the freeing of our African minds. I will always remember them with gratitude and thanks.

The love and encouragement of my twin daughters, Janice and Janet, and their mother, my wife Florie, have given me the strength to carry on in spite of obstacles on the way.

This book was put together with a firm commitment to the African struggle. If there are one or two print flaws they are of negligible importance and do not diminish the significance of the historical information in this volume. What matters most is that this study was written with love. The ancestors will be pleased.

EDWARD SCOBIE

CONTENTS

LIST OF ILLUSTRATIONS

PREFACE

lobal African Presence consists of a collection of lectures given at conferences, articles published in journals, particularly *The Journal of African Civilizations,* and some unpublished works. What the book sets out to show is the presence of Africans, not as enslaved inferiors, but achievers in all realms of human endeavor. It deals also with the continuous battles in which Africans were engaged to liberate themselves totally from the inhumanities of their tormentors. In fact, one could say that the thematic line of *Global African Presence* is empowerment at any and all costs. The words of Harriet Tubman keep echoing throughout the pages: "I wanted to be free. I started with this idea in my head; there's two things I've got a right to, and these are Death or Liberty — one or the other I mean to have. I shall fight for my liberty." The warriors who patrol through these pages, from Queen Nzingha to Queen Mother Moore, Dessalines to Zumbi, carry this ancestral spirit with them.

EDWARD SCOBIE

INTRODUCTION

I have known Professor Edward Scobie for several years. He is among the most remarkable men I have met. In my early days in England as a broadcaster for the B.B.C., he was a legend at Bush House and a name on the lips of radio audiences throughout the English-speaking Caribbean. Both his broadcasting and journalism were distinguished by qualities of style, imagination, and breadth of knowledge equal to any in his field in Britain.

As an editor of Flamingo and other publications, he was admired by millions for his courageous stand on behalf of minorities and by his range of experience and background information on the condition of Blacks throughout what was then the British colonial empire. This vast knowledge, coupled with his considerable dramatic skills, made his radio plays, media events and later culminated in his book, *Black Britannia*. This is the most comprehensive and well-written history of Blacks in the British world and clearly establishes Professor Scobie as a major researcher and historian.

During the difficult years of preparation for my book, *They Came Before Columbus*, Professor Scobie was one of the few scholars who encouraged, advised, and morally supported me. He is, in my estimation, in the class of the Renaissance men - a great teacher, writer, scholar of history and literature, a leader of men, and a loyal and noble friend.

Edward Scobie, author of *Black Britannia*, the most important history so far published on Blacks in the British Isles, presents us with a broad and comprehensive outline of the role of Blacks in the Spanish, Italian, Portuguese, Dutch, French and British worlds, demonstrating their pervasive presence and impact for centuries, their infiltration even into Europe's religious hierarchies and royal families. Brilliant figures like Alexandre Dumas, péré, Alessandro dei Medici, Jacobus Capitein, Black Roman popes and Afro-Portuguese kings flash across the European landscape, startling their times with a personal lightning that triumphed over the prejudice engulfing so many of their despised race.

Among the special essays, of first importance in the field of African civilizations, is "The African Popes." Professor Scobie introduces us to the story of three Black popes of Rome-St. Victor I, St. Miltiades, and St. Gelasius. Most importantly, he, shows us what they really looked like and what they came in the European dominated centuries to look like, as their faces were deliberately altered in order to wipe out from the consciousness of later times the memory of their original African ancestry. The most striking of these visual comparisons may be found in the case of Miltiades: a 9th century fresco of this African pope stands out in sharp contrast with later representations. The implications of this are very disturbing since the official Roman Church must have known of the deception and yet, by the grievous sin of omission or collusion, failed to correct it.

In an even more illuminating essay, Scobie examines the role of the Black woman in early Europe. She occupies extreme positions in the European imagination. She is, on the one hand, the sex goddess and courtesan. The kings and the noblemen of France and Portugal; a cardinal in Italy, later to become a pope; Baudelaire; and Shakespeare, greatest of poets, rush to her bed. She is so irresistible that, in spite of all the racial prejudices of the day, her blood ultimately runs through the royal and noble families of Europe: Queen Charlotte Sophia, the Duke of Florence, the Medicis, the Gonzagas, the Duchess of Alafoes, St. Hilaire, son of Louis XV. The list is great, but the contradiction is greater. For she is virtuous – the Greek goddess of chastity, Artemis, is Black; she is wise – the goddess of wisdom is Minerva, an African princess; she is a saint, as are the Black Madonnas of Loretta in Italy, Nuria in Spain, Czestochowa in Poland.

In his study of the Moors, Edward Scobie also brings into focus these aspects of Moorish science that made the global expansion of Portuguese possible. Why did the British, French, Dutch and Italians who owned the ships not undertake this journey? Since their leaders also possessed the necessary vision for such an enterprise, why didn't they take the lead? The Portuguese jumped ahead because they drew upon everything they could from the Moors. Their geographical lore, for example, since the Muslims traveled the length and breadth of the then-known world and wrote the most meticulous travel accounts (Ibn Battuta and Ibn Hawkel, all the advances in navigation-lateen sails, astrolabes and nautical compasses, astronomical tables, tubes, to the extremities of which ocular and object diopters were attached, the measurement of time by pendulum oscillations, the finest maps. Also, gunpowder and artillery (the Moors had not only made the firestick, but even cannons forged from wrought iron.)

Prince Henry the Navigator (born 1394) gets all the credit for the impetus toward Portugal's expansion as if this was simply a result of his creative genius. The depletion of precious metals in Europe due to the demands of foreign trade and the costly wars that were taking place, leading to even further shortages, pushed Europe to turn to Africa as an untapped source. But it was the science of the Moors that spearheaded European expansion. As Professor Hamilton, quoted by Scobie, puts it, "It was both the lore and lure of Africa."

His essays on the Blacks in Europe – Blacks in the religious and royal hierarchies – as well as the role of the Black woman in antiquity, are the best in the field. Professor Scobie combines a broad and expert knowledge of his subject with the dramatic skill of the rapporteur. This is a rare gift that brings history alive to students. His portrait of the amazingly gifted Chevalier St. Georges, whose brilliance as composer, conductor, violinist, swordsman, equestrian, and soldier took him to the palaces of kings and made him the darling of society, makes a mockery of the baseless fabrications Europeans cling to about the inferiority of African peoples. For make no mistake about it, there have been numerous men and women of African ancestry of equal worth as Chevalier.

The Journal of African Civilizations dedicated its most ambitious issue – *The African Presence in Europe* – to Professor Scobie, because there is no one in the Black world who has done such major pioneering work in this subject.

A substantial part of this book deals with African resistance, particularly during the centuries of slavery. This is something that has been deliberately played down by historians. History books, as a result, have always placed undue prominence on the works of those abolitionists, predominantly Europeans, who campaigned for abolition and emancipation. That is an unjustified statement at the expense of the continuous resistance by the enslaved Africans themselves. Also, Africans have played a significant role in the abolitionist movement. The chapters, "African Resistance to Slavery" and "The Haitian Revolution Re-Examined" bear eloquent testimony to this issue of resistance.

It is perhaps because of his gentleness and graciousness, the lack of aggressive and self-serving ego, that Professor Scobie is not yet fully recognized and rewarded for his work. I would not alter a word of the very high regard I have for his many talents. My respect and admiration for his work has not changed over the years, except to deepen.

DR. IVAN VAN SERTIMA

CHAPTER ONE

The African Diaspora: Research Base For Curricula Content

For centuries, African peoples, both on the Motherland and elsewhere, have suffered one of the worst disasters that western academia ever perpetrated on the minds of millions of those they arrogantly designate "Third World" peoples. They, those imperialists, enslavers, and colonizers, have removed almost totally from our minds the vision of Africa in their deliberate exclusion from the curriculum of schools, beginning at kindergarten level, right through the school stage, up to higher education, and to the graduate university level. It is not an accident of education that this happened, if we listen to the words of one of Britain's most celebrated scholars, Dr. Hugh Trevor-Roper, Regius Professor of History of Oxford University. In a work entitled *The Rise of the Christian Empire* he stated, "undergraduates seduced, as always, by the changing breath of journalistic fashion, demand that they should be taught the history of Black Africa. Perhaps in the future there will be some African history to teach. But at present there is none, or very little. There is only the history of Europeans in Africa, the rest is darkness and darkness is not a subject for history. Men existed even in dark centuries, but to study their history would be to amuse ourselves with the unrewarding gyrations of barbarous tribes in picturesque but irrelevant corners of the globe."

Trevor-Roper is not alone in this calculated racism and

intellectual dishonesty. It has been with us for centuries, ever since Europeans came into contact with Africans and began the systematic practice of exploitation, rape and plunder of them and their continent.

In the eighteenth century, and before, there was a whole corpus of historians like Edward Long, Samuel Estwick and Gilbert Francklyn, who wrote historical diatribes about the inferiority of Africans, comparing them to orangutans, and claiming that the latter came out better in moral and intellectual sensibilities.

Experiments were conducted with slaves to test whether Africans could absorb, retain and profit by a European education. One such guinea pig' was a Jamaican slave named Francis Williams who, after a Cambridge University education and in the face of great obstacles, became a prominent educator on that Caribbean island. These experiments were conducted in spite of the fact that there had already been slave scholars of very high standing like Jacobus Eliza Capitein, who studied at the University of Leyden and earned a degree in philosophy in 1740. He published two works: a treatise on the calling of the Gentiles, De Vocatione Ethnicorum, which ran into three editions; and a book of sermons in Dutch. Juan Latino was an African professor of poetry at the University of Granada in Spain. His remarkable book on Don Juan of Austria at the Battle of Lepanto was published in Granada in 1573, and won him respect as a scholar. It is one of the most prized rare books in the world today.

There were still others like Anthony William Amo, who was born on the coast of Guinea. He studied at the University of Wittenberg at Halle, Saxony, and wrote and spoke fluent Greek, Latin, Hebrew, Dutch, French and German. He obtained his doctorate for a philosophical work called "The Want of Feeling." A second book by Amo was published in

1734. It was also philosophical and dealt with the sensations that involve the mind and the organic workings of the body.

Slavery was only a part, and a comparatively recent part, of the African and his history. Africans had a civilization more ancient than that of Europe, but it has been distorted in the writings of White historians with half-truths, omissions, and outright lies. Franz Fanon himself said that when he "rummaged frenetically through all the antiquity of the Black man," what he found there took away his breath," adding: "I was not primitive, not even a half-man. I belonged to a race that had already been working in gold and silver two thousand years ago."

To find that out and much more, to set the record straight, to wipe out the half-truths and outright lies, to put on record the omissions, to find our rightful place in the history of human race, African scholars have a sacred duty to perform and it is quite simply this: to rewrite our own history, to find out the truth about our heritage, and how it all began. This is what some African scholars and writers have been about, but Europeans still continue to spread their virus of miseducation. They persist in keeping the truth about Africa and Africans out of their Eurocentric curriculum, and thus have confused the minds of generations of African peoples for centuries.

Europeans claim that they spread civilization and its benefits around this planet when all other species of the human family, especially those from the continent of Africa, were in a vacuum of darkness and paganism. That assertion has absolutely no historical, anthropological, or spiritual base on which to stand. In other words, these beliefs are utterly baseless and false. Yet European scholars cling to them with madness that causes them to commit acts of terrorism and genocide against those of other races – particularly Africans – that would disgrace a forest of brute beasts. The persistence and arrogance that Eurocentric scholars use to impose their will on others have endangered not only Africans but indeed the entire planet. That Europeans will themselves be victims has not dawned on them because they are so imprisoned in their fog of White supremacy. They have become blinded with this permanent disease. It is for these reasons that the Eurocentric foundations in western and, in fact, global education, must be removed from curricula, not only on this continent, but in all the other areas of the planet where Europeans have been miseducating non-White peoples into thinking that they have been and will continue to be the inferiors of the world if Europe and its people do not control and define the path that humanity must take.

This is one of the deadliest beliefs with which we are faced today. That is why it is a matter of life or death if African scholars, who are here and elsewhere, do not fight determinedly to change this Eurocentric education into one that meets the requirements of Africans.

First of all, let us examine important studies that Europeans have deliberately erased from the pages of history. They know full well that the studies they used to hang on to their myth of superiority were bereft of authenticity and truth. These fabrications of history have been exposed from the time of Herodotus (484-425 BC) right down to today by scholars ranging from British scholars Basil Davidson and Dr. Martin Bernal; the late Dr. Cheik Anta Diop of Senegal; Dr. Joseph Ben-Jochannon; Dr. John Henrik Clarke; Dr. Asa Hilliard III; Dr. Maulana Karenga; Dr. Leonard Jeffries; Dr. Charsee McIntyre; Dr. Jacob Carruthers; Dr. Ivan Van Sertima, Dr. Charles S. Finch III; and other African and African-American scholars too numerous to mention. In writing why the Egyptians could not be Africoid, Baron G. Cuvier maintained:

The negro race...is marked by black complexion,

crisped or woolly hair, compressed cranium and a flat nose...The projection of the lower parts of the face, and the thick lips, evidently approximate it to the monkey tribe: the hoards of which it consists have always remained in the most complete state of barbarism.

The Comte de Gobineau, that pioneer racist, followed that same path, writing:

The black variety is the lowest and lies at the bottom of the ladder...if its faculties for thinking are mediocre or even nonexistent, it possesses in its desire and as a consequence in its will an intensity that is often terrible. Many of the senses are developed with a vigour unknown in the other two races; principally taste and smell. It is precisely in the greed for sensations that the most striking mark of its inferiority is found.

But times are changing and a renaissance of African scholars has put that mytho-European history to rest.

Africa is now in center stage. Take the Egyptologist James Henry Breasted, whom Dr. Charles S. Finch III described as "dean of American Egyptologists." Dr. Finch launched his onslaught on Breasted's falsification of the African in choice pieces of prose. But before Dr. Finch's criticism is quoted, the statement by Breasted, which caused it must be exposed:

Unfitted by ages of tropical life for any effective intrusion among the white race, the Negro and negroid people remained without any influence on the development of civilization.

And now, Dr. Finch's comments:

Those words by James Henry Breasted, dean of

American Egyptologists echoed the dominant sentiment of the time: that Black Africa had no share in the creation of any of the first civilizations of man. This message was so powerful and so tenacious that as recently as May 31, 1987, Dr. Edward Bleiberg, assistant director of the Institute of Egyptian Art and Archaeology at Memphis State University, stated categorically in the Memphis Commercial Appeal that, "Egyptians were considered Caucasians."

This then, is the crux of the controversy that has flared up repeatedly throughout that 155-year existence of Egyptology. The argument continues today, but in the face of ever increasing evidence that civilization – like the human race itself – began in Africa, the once-prevailing view is clearly doomed.

At this point, it is necessary to show the kind of research base that is important to include in curricula content, if we are to infuse Africa and African-American content into the school curriculum. It will be necessary to deal with African science and technology from the very beginning before the name Europe came into the history books.

One of the mythologies that the western world has hung onto with the arrogance that one comes to expect from imperialist thinking is that science and technology are beyond the capabilities of African minds and that these two areas of learning are the sole concepts of European man. Nothing could be further from the truth. There have been obvious reasons for this belief. Attitudes about the inferiority of Africans and the non-participation of Africans in the scientific knowledge of the world have been created and recorded in the histories written by Europeans. Africans were always made to be beings somewhat less than human. It was very well stated by Ivan Van Sertima when he noted:

Anthropology has had a long love affair with the primitive and has preferred to set its tent down among the African Bushmen, exploring the simplicities of tiny tribal communities rather than the complexities to be found in the primary centers of large African nations. Very partial and limited visions of the African hovering on the fringes of his vast world have come to represent the totality of his capacity and potential. Even notable African scholars, in their romantic embrace of this exotic savage, have come to the conclusion that the African invented nothing, explored nothing, but occupied some special sensory or emotional realm in his experience of the natural world.

Not so very long ago, no work was attempted which gave serious treatment to the technologies of early Africa. When writing about Africa and Africans, European scholars were predisposed to confine their pens within the negative and dehumanizing concepts of the African slave trade and the institution of slavery when millions of Africans were reduced to the non-human state of property. It is only within comparatively recent years that the situation has been changing. This is partly due to the fact that archaeology has revealed the lineaments of a lost African science, at least in areas outside of Egypt. Again, it has only been fairly recently that the discovery of a seminal Black kingdom in the Nile Valley, predating the Egyptian dynasties, has settled once and for all the question of the roots of classical Egyptian culture and technology.

Since that time, evidence has been unearthed in several fields of science in Africa – agricultural and pastoral science, architecture, aeronautics, engineering, mathematics, mining, metallurgy, medicine, navigation and physics – that has shaken the pristine chambers of European scholarship. These astonishing discoveries in the fields just mentioned have caused a completely new long look at Africa. Previously the nerve of the world has been deadened for centuries to the capacity and heights to which African achievements had reached, and reached long before Europe could lay claim to civilization. This fact caused Van Sertima to observe:

> Every new revelation has made us realize that the eyes of the anthropologist and historian have been focusing on the edge or periphery of the African world, blind to all that has lain within the heartland of its civilization.

These revelations about Africa's knowledge of science, which were revealed to the world, exposed falsehoods that were in current and wide usage for these past five centuries. Since that time of exposure we have seen the discovery of African steel smelting in Tanzania 1,500-2000 years ago; an astronomical observatory in Kenya 300 years before Christ; the cultivation of cereals and other crops by Africans in the Nile Valley 7,000 years ago, before any other civilization; the domestication of cattle in Kenya 15,000 years ago; the domestic use of fire by Africans 1,400,000 years ago (one million years before its first known use in China); the use of tetracycline by an ancient African population fourteen centuries ago; an African glider-plane 2,300 years old; a probe by microwave beams of an American radar satellite beneath the sands of the Sahara, revealing cultures 200,000 years old and the traces of ancient rivers running from this African center. Some of the buried stream valleys appear to be "ancient connections to the Upper Nile tributaries," toward which Blacks migrated, later populating Nubia and Egypt.

What has caused this almost total disappearance of the science and technology of Africa? The answer is not too difficult to find. We can conclude, without any fear of contradiction, that no human disaster can equal in dimension of destructiveness the cataclysm that shook Africa. Everyone is familiar with the slave trade and the traumatic effect of this on the transplanted Black, but very few realize what horrors were brought down on the continent of Africa itself. Vast populations were uprooted and displaced; entire generations totally disappeared; European maladies descended like the plague, decimating both cattle and people; cities and towns were abandoned; family networks vanished like the desert air; kingdoms crumbled; and finally, the threads of culture and historical continuity were so ruthlessly torn asunder that from that time, one would think of only two Africas: the one prior to and the one after the Holocaust of the slave trade, slavery and all that these two tragedies entailed.

Anthropologists have claimed that 80% of traditional African culture survived. What they meant to say when they used the word "traditional" was that the only kind of culture we have come to accept as African is that of the primitive on the periphery, the stunned survivor. However, the African genius was not to remain buried forever. Five centuries later, archaeologists, digging among the ruins, began to pick up some of the pieces. These pieces illustrate quite clearly that Africans, as the first humans on planet Earth, were the originators of the sciences and technology.

It is with this important knowledge in mind that we must work towards the twenty-first century, using African brains to put science and technology to work for the benefit of Africans and the African continent, for Africans anywhere and everywhere on this planet.

Too often has the imperialist taunt been thrown at us that Africa is underdeveloped. We know why this has been so and it is up to each and every one of the sons and daughters of Africa to rectify that situation. It is one of the ironies that the continent with all the minerals and natural resources to maintain a good life for its people is the one that still remains, at the approach of another century, underdeveloped. This brings to mind a story that has been repeated by a Nigerian, time and time again. The emotions which welled up in him when telling this tale were those of frustration and anger caused when this young schoolboy would see the hundreds of cargo boats of Europe and North America leaving the dockside, packed to capacity with the oil and other mineral resources of Nigeria, and beginning their return journey across the Atlantic. This young man knew that valuable resources of his continent were being taken to build scientific and technological wealth of the same countries that had enslaved Africans and plundered their land. This is still being done. Constitutional independence of African nations does not seem to have changed this condition. It would seem that the economic face of Africa, unlike the political face, still remains White. The countries of this mineral-rich continent can never gain the supreme power and control of their affairs as long as Africa is allowed to remain in this state of underdevelopment.

The sons and daughters of the continent possess, in abundance and ever-growing numbers, the training, expertise and experience in the fields of science and technology to turn their capabilities in that direction. No one but Africans can bring Africa to the power and glory that it rightly deserves. Here the word "Africans" is used in the way the late brilliant, visionary scholar Cheik Anta Diop would, to encompass Africans everywhere on the planet. It would be naïve to expect those imperial countries to want to remove Africa from its underdevelopment and make it a strong, powerful continent. The colonizers, at no time of their thinking, ever had that intention in mind. They do not have it today neither will they have it tomorrow.

A former United States president once said "Africa is very important to us, to our survival. We need her oil and her other resources. To allow Russia to get the upper hand in Africa will put our way of life in danger." Others share that thinking. They will always want to take from Africans, and even retake Africa for themselves. It is an age-old colonial custom.

Too many Africans are unaware of the major contributions of Blacks to modern technology. In 1913 alone, as many as 1,000 inventions were patented by African Americans. They were the lucky ones who managed to get as far as the patent office. In the previous century several Africans who were enslaved on the cotton concentration camps of the South invented laborsaving devices but were not allowed to patent them in their own names. In the year 1858 the Attorney General of the United States ruled that since a patent was a contract between the government and the inventor, and since a slave was not considered a United States citizen, he could not make a contract with the government.

In spite of these oppressive and inhospitable circumstances, there was no total loss of African ingenuity and technological innovation. Van Sertima analyzed this condition very succinctly when he wrote:

> The thread of African genius began to unravel, like light speeding through the spools of the glass fibre light guides black scientist Northover developed. Or like impulses travelling along the transatlantic cable Richardson helped to lay down, channeling voices from one continent to another, one time to another, bridging the chasm between the ancestral African and the modern African, between root and branch, seed and flower, an old heart and a new brain.

These remarks are from a historian with a love and passion for science and technology who realizes, like every colleague, that these will open the gates of true liberation for Africa. Was it not one of our great leaders, Marcus Mosiah

Garvey, who said that the nation that produces men and women of science, will one day play a significant part in the control of world affairs? We will not be beggars anymore from those who have shown themselves to be our enemies, or, if you prefer, enemies to our development for centuries and centuries. Metaphorically, Africa must turn on the light that Lewis Latimer gave to the world and for which a European, Edison, has reaped the rewards and the glory. Let that never, never again happen.

Africa for Africans at home and abroad, as our brother, Marcus Mosiah Garvey, shouted to us year after year after year: we must heed that clarion call, and very quickly. African educators have a dual task to perform: one, to expunge all the distortions, myths, perjuries, half-truths, and false claims from the Eurocentric curriculum that have poisoned the minds of generations of Africans wherever they live on this planet. Europeans must not be allowed to inhabit center stage in the global history of the world. Why? Simply because they were not there in the remote centuries, when Africans walked this planet. Not to put Africa in that spot is to pervert the course of history and to place the origins of the early civilizations in the hands of those who had no hand in their creation. Secondly, African educators, after having performed this cleansing, must re-write and produce a curriculum in tune and in truth with the happenings in the long history of Africans as the originators of world civilization. This, as we can see, is a monumental task. It is something we owe to ourselves and, more particularly, to our children growing up to meet the challenges of the next generation. If we do not set about this duty with alacrity it may even be too late by the turn of the century. In an "Editor's Note" in the New York University magazine Brownstone it was well stated: "When children are denied their culture, they lose an emotional and psychological foundation that is vital to their sense of self-esteem, self-worth and self-love." We see the result of a lack of these three qualities all around us: in Riker's Island, in the crack-ridden streets and teenagers in various stages of pregnancy.

In spite of all these and other dangers that we face, in societies that are dominated by Europe we still behave in a manner that liberation from our oppression will come from those who have oppressed us for these last five hundred years. In 1992 we paid homage to a man who lost himself on the high seas, found himself in this hemisphere and set in motion mass genocide of the Arawaks and Caribs; and later being instrumental in bringing Africans to these parts to perform the labor that the Arawaks and Caribs would not or did not perform. We spent that year of 1992 in an orgy of excesses celebrating a man whose crimes against us would bring beasts in the forest to shame. What this grandiose celebration means is that European history is going to follow the same path as of yore, and that little fragments of Africa will be fitted in to fill the fringes and play its usual minor role in the happenings of the world. In other words, it will remain in the same place it occupied before in its contribution to world civilizations: hidden at the bottom of the barrel, too insignificant to be seen and observed.

We cannot keep on pointing to the oppressor, expecting him or her to educate and cultivate not only our minds but those of our children. The time has come to change this flawed strategy; there is an utter madness in this method. In a society that rarely allows an individual more than one chance to receive a "quality education," to do nothing in the face of madness is to condemn many of our brothers and sisters to a harsh and brutal life.

Yet European scholars hang on to claims that Europe is their inspiration. That may be so, but it has brought precious little inspiration to the sons and daughters of Africa, wherever they may be in the world. Some may even state that it brought none at all. Africans see Europe not as the messenger of civilization and culture. Europe, to them signifies oppression, even genocide; the perpetrators of imperialism, enslavement, colonialism and the other negatives which plague Africans everywhere. In an opinion column in the Daily News of Tuesday, December 19, 1989, writer George F. Will puts the seal on spreading the miseducation that Europe has been doing for these hundreds of years. He writes:

> " Eurocentricity" is right, in American curriculums and consciousness, because it accords with the facts of our history, and we–and Europe– are fortunate for that. The political and moral legacy of Europe has made the most happy and admirable nations. Saying that may be indelicate, but it has the merit of being true, and the truth should be the core of any curriculum.

George F. Will was wrong: what he said was not indelicate. It was the mouthing of a man seriously diseased with the illness of White supremacy. This has certainly not been the case in the curriculum that Europe has imposed on African people. It is precisely the reason we are fighting tooth and nail to change it. Our survival, and that of our children, is in danger if we do not keep on struggling until we succeed in this academic battle.

When Dr. Leonard Jeffries, Jr., a PhD from Columbia University, argues strongly for an African-centered curriculum, they ridicule his claims. What he says at its most basic means teaching children not just about Benjamin Franklin but also about his contemporary, the Black astronomer and mathematician Benjamin Banneker; not just about Thomas Edison but also about Lewis Latimer, the Black scientist who developed the carbon filament without which Edison's electric lights would burn only 16 hours; not just about ancient Greece and Rome, but also their remarkable roots in African civilization. These facts have been stated time and time again by Jeffries. They were included in a document by Maynard

Eaton titled African American Affirmation: Ice vs. Sun Theory. Maynard Eaton went on to say:

> It means revolutionizing the nation's classrooms by teaching students the view of (Dr.) Jeffries and like-minded scholars that the history of Europe and America is one of oppression of people of color, continuing to the present day.

For that stance, Jeffries has been pilloried by lesser intellects with all sorts of idiotic and senseless phrases like "foolish diatribe," "intellectual absurdities," and "weak-kneed scholarship." That kind of criticism does not have half a leg to stand on. What they cannot stomach is his well-researched scholarship and the depth and strength of his analysis. As he has said time and time again, "nothing will stop me from my sacred mission". There is a fast-growing school of scholars who are with Jeffries in that great mission.

Lerone Bennett Jr., author of *Before the Mayflower*, once stated that, "An educator in a system of oppression is either a revolutionary or an oppressor." This great surge in fighting for a curriculum that addresses itself in such a way that we can identify ourselves in a very positive way means that we have changed our position and have become revolutionaries. This stance should have been taken ages ago, for, in the words of Frederick Douglass, "Power concedes nothing without a struggle. It never did. It never will." One of the most glaring problems of the African American community is that for all our movements and organizing, we have yet to form a viable internal coalition which would address a major issue in our lives and the lives of our children: education. It is only now, at this moment in time, that we have taken up intellectual arms. Although our forces are growing there is still a sizeable proportion of Negro scholars – and I use this description deliberately – who are either hanging on the fence, still bending on the side of European miseducation, or those who prefer to fight side by side with the oppressors.

We have set out to define a curriculum of inclusion, which is in fact an Africana curriculum. It will be drafted and put in the hands of Africans everywhere, whether the Board of Education turns it down or not. We positively refuse to take our children into the next century with a curriculum of exclusion still based on the fabrications of race supremacists. Our Africana curriculum is being designed to present the totality of the African world experience from its roots in Africa; the origin of humankind to the development of Civilization in the Nile Valley and Ethiopia, through the destructive impact of the slave system and its aftermath the transatlantic distribution of Blacks throughout the Americas. The course material of this curriculum will reflect an analysis of the continuity of the Black Experience within the context of the African world. It also will provide a conceptual framework for comparing the experiences of African people within the European American world as well as with the Latin and Asian and Caribbean world.

A curriculum of this nature and magnitude must include the Caribbean. As African peoples, or if you prefer to describe them, as people of African descent, they share fundamental qualities in culture, religious beliefs, song, dance, and way of life with African Americans and with Africans on the motherland. All share the horrors of European oppression. Any curriculum that deals with Africana Studies in the college classroom, must include Caribbean Studies. Africana Studies covers that body of knowledge about Africans from the dawn of civilization to the present. That "body of knowledge" encompasses not only Africans on the mainland continent but Africans everywhere in the Diaspora. Although the experiences of Africans in this hemisphere are fundamentally similar; slavery, being common to all the regions– North, Central and South America, and the Caribbean–in all its linguistic dimensions, yet each geopolitical area needs to be dealt with, in detail, linking it to the collective experience.

To begin with, the inclusion of Africana Studies–or Black Studies as it was once commonly known in the college curriculum–has been a comparatively recent phenomenon, a mere two decades, or so, ago. And it came to pass under political pressures from the civil rights struggles of the sixties. Since that time it has been treated as the odd man out or, perhaps, the unwanted child of academia. Caribbean Studies, then, within that context, has been viewed in an even more unfavorable light in the academic world. Curiously enough, this attitude, until only recently, was very much in evidence even in the region of the Caribbean itself. Professor Gordon K. Lewis, in his study *Slavery, Imperialism, and Freedom,* made this observation pointedly when he wrote:

> Up to the present moment Latin American, studies, not to speak, say, of Caribbean Studies, continue to suffer a subordinate status in the universities … There has been, as it were, a chronic failure on the part of the English people to develop a cosmic view of things. Public opinion, both popular and educated, has remained dismally unaware of the fact that what is called "Western Civilization" has always been only one culture from among a global host of non-European "civilization" and that many of those other civilizations have been possessed of a historical antiquity predating the Western forms by centuries.

Oftentimes it has been said that Caribbean peoples, up to this point in time, suffer from a condition of "pastlessness". That malady has come about by a denial, or an absence, of Africa in their lives. Strangely enough, those "pastless" ones have built their lives on the false assumptions of their European masters. It is this sad state of being which caused Dr. C.L.R. James to observe in his preface to classical study of Toussaint

L'Ouverture and the St. Dominique Revolution titled, *The Black Jacobins*:

> Writers of the West Indies always relate them [Caribbean peoples] to their approximation to Britain, France, Spain and America; that is to say, to Western civilization, never in relation to their own history.

Some writers go even further in their abysmal lack of the true cultural values of Caribbean peoples, of whom over 85% are of African descent. This state, ironically, is very much in evidence even to this day. In a recent novel, the African Caribbean writer, Maryse Conde, makes one of the characters speak scornfully about the Caribbean past in which she was born:

> Don't you know that history never bothered about niggers? It's been proven they weren't worth the fuss. They had no part in building the Golden Gate Bridge or the Eiffel Tower, instead of praying at Notre Dame or Westminster Abbey, they knelt before a piece of wood, bowed down to a snake. A snake, can you imagine?...You might think everybody has a history. Well no. These people have none.

Vidia (VS) Naipaul, the Trinidad Indian, whose eyes have been blinkered by the bile of colonialism, spews forth in his historical travelogue, *The Middle Passage*, these archaic racial words, once heard from as "mad dogs and Englishmen" once besotted by rum and the noonday sun of Empire: "The history of these islands can never be satisfactorily told. Brutality is not the only difficulty. History is built around achievement and creation; and nothing was created in the West Indies."

The inclusion of Caribbean Studies in Africana Studies

is imperative, not only for those in Caribbean lands, but also for Africans everywhere. The lack of knowledge of their true selves as African peoples has been catastrophic. It is still the popular belief that the millions of Africans transported against their will to the Caribbean in chains had nothing to begin with, and created nothing since arrival. It still happens to be the case – in the words of anthropologist Eric Wolf, "that they and their descendants constitute a vanguard for those people to whom history has too often been denied."

This denial of history has come, ironically, from scholars in opposing ideological camps and with contrasting traditions of historical inquiry. Imperial historians, whose writings until recently permeated not only the standard scholarly interpretations of the Caribbean past but also the schoolbooks of Caribbean children, saw the Caribbean primarily as a theater of wars between the great powers for possession of the territorial lands. It was no wonder that the history of the area and the African peoples there were seen from the perspectives of Westminster, Madrid, the Hague or the Quai d'Orsay. In this version of history, the African Caribbean peoples appeared very seldom, if at all. When they did appear, they were treated as pawns in the colonial setting, being moved about at the will of the imperialists. This has had a negative effect on generations of African peoples in the Caribbean and, indeed, on Africans everywhere. It is precisely this negativity regarding studies about the Caribbean in relation to African roots that we seek to remove. The consequences of this kind of history are accurately noted by poet Derek Walcott in his anthology, *Another Life*:

> I saw history through the sea-washed eyes
> of our choleric ginger-haired headmaster
> beak like an inflamed hawk's
> a lonely Englishman
> who loved parades
> sailing, and Conrad's prose.

Finally, there is another idea widespread among North American, European and Caribbean intellectuals that African-Caribbean peoples suffer from a profound lack of historical consciousness; they know nothing and couldn't care less about their own complex, and, at times, often unhappy past.

Richard Price, in a study he called *An Absence of Ruins*, argues that:

> The process of colonialism has so whitewashed Caribbean minds that history has come to mean only 1066, Waterloo, and "nos ancestres gaulois." About their own history, the argument goes, rural Caribbean peoples are abysmally even adamantly ignorant, having successfully forgotten the horrors that their ancestors suffered.

I have gone to great lengths to discuss this issue of historical "pastlessness" among African Caribbean peoples because it has been the cause for much divisiveness, ignorance and hypocrisy among those of the area, even to this day. The notion that African culture and learning began only from slavery on cotton plantations and sugar cane estates is still voiced, even by African men who should know better, like Dr. Thomas Sowell in his strange misleading study titled *Ethnic America*.

Thus, the curriculum of Africana Studies that includes Caribbean Studies – as it must – needs to be designed to present the totality of the African experience and heritage. So, it must begin with the dawn of mankind on the continent of Africa, and the very beginnings of civilization. For, make no mistake about it, it was Africa that gave civilization to the world. It is from that point, and with that concept that Caribbean Studies, within the rubric of Africana Studies, must be approached and taught. For Africana Studies, while incorporating and encouraging specialization in one or more subject areas like the Caribbean, Brazil, Latin America, requires as a coherent discipline and the linking of these subject areas within it, to be overall principles and fundamental thrusts of the discipline.

Africana Studies is the scientific study of the dimensional aspects of Black thought and practice in their current and historical unfolding. Thus we must define Africana Studies as a social science, and, in consort with all other social sciences, it possesses its own specific focus on human relations and behavior. Whereas the economist is preoccupied with economic matters and the political scientist with the affairs of politics, Africana Studies in all its areas must begin its focus of inquiry and analysis on Africana thought and behavior. Africana thought and practice (or behavior) being such an inclusive focus is of necessity bound to be interdisciplinary – inclusive of, and informed by many disciplines.

It is absolutely important to state here and now, that to teach an introductory course in Caribbean Studies, or any other course within the discipline of Africana Studies, calls for a completely different approach. In other words, a Eurocentric view must be replaced by an African-centered one. In plain words, Africa and African peoples must be placed at center stage. To do that will mean treading on many historical corns. Misconceptions, mythologies, half-truths, fantasies, and outright lies will have to be scratched from the pages of European histories about Africana peoples, histories which have dehumanized Africans and can only be described as racist.

Today, one does not have to resort to books by historians and others from metropolitan countries, to teach Africana Studies in the Caribbean or any other area. Black scholars have produced major definitive works on almost, or nearly all, aspects of Africana Studies. There have been very few European and American scholars who have written with honesty and truth about Africans on this planet. In fact, some

27

of the writings by European scholars have been objectionable and almost an insult to scholarship, not to mention a gross disservice to African peoples. But that is nothing new.

No course in Caribbean Studies can begin with the Caribbean area. Since the large numbers of Caribbean peoples (25 million) are of African origin, then for purposes of historical identity and origin we must start in Africa. Equally important is the fact that African history is an essential of world history. In fact, there is no way to be knowledgeable about world history without an understanding of African history. So, all courses in every area of Africana Studies are designed to destroy the concept of Africa as the "dark and savage" continent, and to restore the African's place in history. This entails a re-examination of African history and an assessment of the reasons for its distortion, providing the basis of a total historical reconstruction. These courses, as I have noted previously, must be taught from an African-centered point of view, using a wide variety of books and documents prepared by scholars of African descent in Africa, Latin America, the Caribbean, Brazil and the United States.

Data and scientific information must be found and used to support the truths being uncovered about the African world experience and its impact on humanity: from the dawn of human development, millions of years ago in East Africa; through the evolution of society 100,000 years ago; to the cradle of civilization in the Nile Valley, 10,000 years ago; up to the diffusion of civilization to other cultures like the Ancient Hebrews and Greeks in 1500 B.C.; down to Medieval Period of Islamic African civilization circa 1000 A.D.; to the Dark Ages' independence in African consciousness renaissance. All the data and documents must contain issues that relate to key concepts in the education and enlightenment of African peoples. These issues must deal with the socialization process; assimilation and acculturation; material and spiritual empowerment; slavery and imperialism; colonialism and neocolonialism; racism and classism; capitalism and fascism; physical and cultural genocide; and African consciousness and African ascension.

In the Caribbean area there are many myths and perjuries to cast by the wayside of history, starting with that controversial navigator, Christopher Columbus, who, apart from uttering and writing many untruths about Caribbean peoples of whom he knew nothing, set out on an orgy of genocide against the Indians (Tainos, Arawaks and Caribs). Then he followed the slave trade and slavery, which caused the extermination of millions and also kept millions in servitude for close to five hundred years. The effects still remain to plague the Caribbean, as noted by Professor Rex Nettleford, head of the Trade Union Education Institute at the University of the West Indies in Mona, Jamaica:

> Cultural penetration and intellectual domination have, however, become current buzzwords in any critique of the new dispensation of a Caribbean which is still struggling to decolonize itself from three centuries of transplantation, exploitation and psychic disrepair.

To repair these conditions and to resurrect the true African from the debris and destruction of slavery and colonialism is the sacred mission of not only Caribbean Studies but all other areas of Africana Studies. This is not only a classroom exercise, but also a lifetime undertaking. A Caribbean inclusion within an Africana curriculum that meets the needs of the people may be eclectic, speculative and certainly controversial, precisely because of the peculiar factors that characterize the region. The same claims can be made for Africans in all parts of the Diaspora and the African continent, the source and foundation of world history and civilization. Not to take this path is to court disaster.

Let me end with a quotation by Dr. Chancellor Williams which illuminates all that I have written so far and believe, with the strength of the feather of Truth handed down to us by ancestors in Kemet thousands of years ago:

"What became of the Black People of Sumer?" the traveller asked the old man, "For ancient records show that the people of Sumer were Black. What happened to them?"
"Ah" the old man sighed. "They lost their history, so they died. . ."

REFERENCES:

Bernal, Martin. *Black Athena.* (New Jersey: Rutgers University Press, 1987)

James, C. L. R. *The Black Jacobins.* (London: Allison & Busby,1980)

Lewis, Gordon K. *Slavery, Imperialism and Freedom* (Monthly Review Press, New York 1978)

Finch III, Charles S. "The Works of Gerald Massey." *Studies in Kamite Origins, Journal of African Civilization* (New Jersey: November, 1982)

Walcott, Derek. *Another Life* (London: Jonathan Cape)

Naipaul V.S. *The Middle Passage,* (London: Andre Deutsch, 1962)

Trevor-Roper, Hugh. *The Rise of the Christian Empire* (New York: Harcourt Brace,1967)

Finch III, Charles. *Great Black Leaders, Vol. 9* (New Jersey: 1987)
Williams, Chancellor. *The Destruction Of Black Civilizations — Great Issues Of A Race from 4500 B.C. to 2000 A.D.* (Chicago: Third World Press, 1976)

CHAPTER TWO

African Popes

In his book, *The Saints Go Marching In*, Robert Fulton Holtzclaw, M.A., made a very important statement in the preface:

> Roman Africa was Roman in name and government, but not in population. The names of the gods and people became Latinized because Latin was the language of the masters of commerce. But the majority of the people were black and the Punic language was spoken until the Islamic invasion in the Eighth Century.

African influence was far-reaching in those very early times. The earliest and most renowned authors in Rome were African, from Terrence to Apuleius. Several of the early saints of the Church were Africans. Robert Holtzclaw throws further light on the darkness of the minds of European scholarship, on the question of Africans and their contributions to Western thought, art, music, religion, when he recorded this fact that:

> Africa did its part in the spiritual history of mankind. One of the most zealous churches of early Christianity came into being in Africa. From Africa came Neo-Platonic thought and the first experiments in monastism. Three of the early popes were black: St. Gelasius, Miltides and Victor I.

This work of research throws further light and examines the lives of these three African popes in greater detail and with more exactitude. They occupied the Papal Chair between the second and fifth centuries, A.D., and made significant contributions to the growth of Christianity and the development of the Roman Catholic Faith. Holtzclaw emphasizes this fact:

> They were Africans and they contributed immeasurably to the, propagation of the Gospel and the establishment, of the Kingdom of God on earth.

It needs to be noted at the outset that pictures of the three African popes in libraries and art galleries, like those of African saints, are not reliable and are not exact color or race likenesses or representations. They were painted from the imagination of the artists, who were European. A case in point is the picture of St. Augustine painted by the Renaissance artist, Sandros Botticelli, in the fifteenth century. Holtzclaw wrote of this painting:

> This great black doctor of the Church lived in the Fifth Century. Notice the aquiline nose and European features.

This same observation can be applied to the African popes whose images were Europeanized, particularly the one of Pope Gelasius I in the Portrait Archive of the Austrian National Library in Vienna. It needs to be observed, too, that the three Popes bore Latin names, as did most Africans there at that time.

That Easter Day is always celebrated on a Sunday, and that the liturgical language of the Roman Catholic Church is Latin are due to the decision of Pope Victor I – the fourteenth in line after Saint Peter. Pope Victor I, although an African, the date and actual region of his birth are unknown. His father's name has been given as Felix. When he ascended the Papal Chair in 189 A.D., the date of Easter continued to be a matter of controversy. In fact, it got very acute. Many of the Christians in Rome who had come from the province of Asia were accustomed to observe Easter on the fourteenth day of the moon. That was the day on which the Jews had been commanded to kill the lamb. It was necessary to finish the fast on that day, whatever day of the week it might be. Instead of recognizing Good Friday as the day of the Lord's death, the Asiatic Christians kept the Jewish feast on the fourteenth day after the new moon with which the month Nisan began. For that reason, they were called Quartodecimans.

Victor I found it disturbing to have one set of Christians observing the fast of Lent and commemorating Christ's passion while other Christians were joyously celebrating the feast of the Resurrection. He was determined to put a stop to this and to bring about unity in observing the Easter festival. With that in view, he set about persuading the Quartodecimans to join in the general practice of the Church. First, he ordered Polycrates, Bishop of Ephesus, to hold a council of Asiatic bishops and get them to follow the Western custom. Headed by Polycrates, the Asiatic bishops met in council. Polycrates then addressed their decision to Victor I and the Church of Rome.

Upon receiving the document from Polycrates, Pope Victor I called a meeting of Italian bishops in Rome. This is the earliest Roman synod on record. He also wrote to the leading Bishops of the various districts, urging them to call together the bishops of their sections of the country and to take counsel with them on the question of the Easter festival. Letters came from all sides: from the synod in Palestine, at which Theophilus of Caesarea and Narcissus of Jerusalem presided; from the synod of Pontus, over which Palmas, as the oldest, presided; from the communities in Gaul whose bishop was Irenaeus of Lyons; from the bishops of the Kingdom of Osrhoene; also from individual bishops, as Bakchylus of Corinth. These letters all unanimously reported that their Easter was observed on

Sunday.

Pope Victor I now called upon the bishops of Asia to abandon their old custom and accept the practice of the majority by celebrating Easter on Sunday. If they failed to abide by his ruling, Victor I declared he would excommunicate all the Christians of Asia. This declaration brought forth swift comment from the bishops, notably Irenaeus of Lyons. Irenaeus wrote to the Pope suggesting reasons why he should not be so harsh with the Asian Christians, strengthening his argument for tolerance of the decision of the Asian bishops by listing high Church dignitaries who did not celebrate Easter on Sunday. In summing up his case Irenaeus showed that his main concern was for a unified church, even though customs among Christians differed. Unfortunately, there is no record to show whether Pope Victor I relented towards the province of Asia in the face of this lengthy and strong plea by Irenaeus. All that is known is in the course of the third century, the Roman practice of observing Easter on a Sunday became gradually universal. In fact, it spread throughout the East. In Rome itself, Pope Victor I naturally saw to it that Easter was celebrated on that day.

While Victor I was Pope, the Church of Rome was plagued by many troubles and troublemakers. One who flouted Victor's Easter Day ruling was an Oriental named Blastus. He started a little church of his own and managed to get a few followers. However, it did not gain footing among the Roman Christians and eventually petered out. Trouble arose, too, during Victor's pontificate, when a rich Christian named Theodotus, a leather merchant from Byzantium, arrived in Rome and began to preach Adoptianism. Theodotus taught that Jesus was a man born of a Virgin according to the counsel of the Father; at His baptism the Spirit – which Theodotus called the Christ – came down upon Him in the likeness of a dove. The Adoptianists did not admit that this made Him God, but some of them said He was God after His Resurrection.

Straightway the Pope condemned this heresy and excluded Theodotus from the Church. The leather merchant would not submit and formed a small sect that lasted for a while in Rome and eventually died out. Victor I was an energetic and zealous pontiff who served the Church of Rome with unswerving faith, even though his firmness in certain issues, notably the Easter controversy, made him somewhat unpopular with certain bishops. He died in 199 A.D. and was buried in the Vatican near St. Peter's. Although nothing is known of the circumstances of his death he is venerated as a martyr, and his feast is kept on July the 28th. Today, in the history of the Roman Church, he is remembered not only for his ruling that Easter should be celebrated on Sunday, but he has also been named in the canon of the Ambrosian Mass, and said by Saint Jerome to have been the first in Rome to celebrate the Holy Mysteries in Latin.

Whereas the pontificate of the first African, Victor I, was rife with troubles for the Church, that of the second, Miltiades, was relatively calmer. He became Pope in 311 A.D. and was the thirty-second pope after St. Peter. He worked tirelessly to ensure that the Church would enjoy a period of peace. An edict of toleration signed by the Emperors Galerius, Licinius and Constantine put an end to the great persecution of the Christians. They were allowed to practice their religion and they could come out of the catacombs where they used to live. Captives were freed from the prisons and mines. Only in those countries of the Orient, which were under the sway of Maximinus Daia, did the Christians continue to be persecuted. However, Emperor Maxentius gave Pope Miltiades in Rome the right to receive back, through the prefect of the city, all ecclesiastical buildings and possessions that had been confiscated during the persecutions. The two Roman deacons, Strato and Cassianus, were ordered by the Pope to discuss this matter with the prefect and to take over the Church properties. It thus became possible to re-organize thoroughly the ecclesiastical administrations and the religious life of the Christians in Rome.

Although Miltiades ruled the Church for only three years, his pontificate witnessed one of history's turning points – the coming of Constantine and the end of the era of persecution. Constantine had been proclaimed Emperor in Gaul, and now in 312 he marched on Rome to overthrow the tyrant Maxentius. His conversion to Christianity had come about when he saw the crucifix in a vision and interpreted it to mean: "By this sign shalt thou conquer."

And he did. The Army of Maxentius was routed at the Milvian Bridge on October the 27th, 312. Peace had come to the Church. Christians throughout the Roman Empire were free. The new Emperor presented the Roman Church with the Lateran Palace. It became the papal residence and the center of administration for the Roman Church. The basilica became the Cathedral of Rome. But, amidst these rejoicings the Church was disturbed by the beginnings of the Donatist schism in Africa. The Donatists claimed that the validity of the sacraments depended on the moral character of the Minister and that sinners could not be members of the true Church nor tolerated by her unless their sins were secret. This disturbance arose when Caecilian was appointed Bishop of Carthage. The Donatists held that his consecration was invalid because he had delivered up the Sacred Books under persecution. Constantine wrote to Miltiades about this matter:

> It appears that Caecilian, the Bishop of the city of the Carthaginians, is called to account on many charges by some of his colleagues in Africa; and in as much as it seems to me to be a very serious matter that in those provinces the multitude should be found pursuing the worse course of action, splitting up, as it were, and the bishops at variance among themselves: It seemed good to me that

36

Caecilian himself, with ten bishops, who seem to call him to account, and such ten others as he may deem necessary to his suit, should set sail for Rome, that there a hearing may be granted him in the presence of yourself, and in such a manner as ye may perceive to be in accordance with the most sacred law. May the Divinity of the great God preserve you safely for many years.

In October, 313, there assembled in the Lateran Palace, under the presidency of Miltiades, a synod of fifteen bishops from Italy and three from Gaul. After considering the Donatist controversy for three days, the synod decided in favor of Caecilian, whose election and consecration as Bishop of Carthage was declared to be legitimate. Saint Augustine spoke about Miltiades in this connection: "An excellent pontiff, a true son of peace and father of Christians."

Miltiades died shortly after the conflict with the Donatists. The date of his death is given as the 10th or 11th of January in 314 A.D. Like Saint Victor I, Miltiades was canonized and is a saint. A commemoration is made of him in the liturgy of December 10 as a martyr because, says the Roman Martyrology, he suffered many things during the persecution of Maximinus before he was Bishop of Rome.

The forty-ninth pope after Saint Peter, Gelasius I, has been described by a contemporary thusly: "Famous all over the world for his learning and holiness." Another says, "More a servant than a sovereign." Yet a third states, "In his private life Gelasius was, above all, conspicuous for his spirit of prayer, penance and study. He took great delight in the company of monks."

Gelasius I was born in Rome of African parents. He took office in the year 492 A.D. Although his pontificate was a short one, he showed himself to be a man of vigor who could speak firmly to the Emperor Anastasius about the need for church independence. He stated:

> The Faith confessed by the Apostolic See is unshakable. It is impossible that it should suffer the taint of false doctrine, or the contact of any error. You must know that the world is governed by two great powers: that of the Popes and that of Kings, but the authority of the Popes is so much the greater inasmuch as on Judgment Day they will have to render an account to God for the souls of Kings. When a pronouncement has come from the Blessed Peter's See no one may question his decision. One can appeal to him from all quarters of the world, but from his decision there is no appeal.

It has been claimed by high-church dignitaries that no one had spoken with loftier eloquence of the greatness of the See occupied by the Popes, than Gelasius I. On other occasions, Gelasius I showed firm belief in the Chair of St. Peter. In writing to the patriarch Euphemius, who wanted to heal the breach in the Church of Constantinople, which was being upheld, by the Emperor, Anastasius I, Gelasius I declared:

> We shall certainly come to the great judgment-seat of Christ, brother Euphemius, surrounded by those by whom the faith has been defended. It will there be proved whether the glorious confession of St. Peter has been lacking anything for the salvation of those given him to rule, or whether there has been rebellion and obstinacy in those who were unwilling to obey him.

Being intelligent and energetic, Gelasius I knew what steps he should take to establish a secure future for the Church. He saved Rome from famine and was emphatic on the duty of bishops to devote a quarter of their revenue to charity, stressing that "Nothing is more becoming to priestly office than the protection of the poor and the weak." Of a bishop that was overly generous with his charity, Gelasius I remarked, "It is little wonder that he died empty-handed as a result of his lavish charity. He used to call his temporal goods: the Patrimony of the poor."

Although Gelasius I was a staunch upholder of old traditions, he nevertheless knew when to make exceptions or modifications, such as his decree insisting on Communion in both kinds. This was done in order to detect the Manichaean heretics, who, though present in Rome in large numbers, attempted to shift attention from their hidden beliefs by pretending to practice true Catholicism. As the heretics held wine to be impure and essentially sinful, they would refuse the chalice and thus be recognized.

At home, Gelasius I did not have much trouble with the imperial government. His difficulty came from a group of wealthy and superstitious Romans. A plague had afflicted the city and these superstitious citizens, led by the Senator Andromachus, wanted to revive the Lupercalia to bring good luck to the city:

> The Lupercalia was originally a pagan rite celebrated in mid-February, but it became a good luck superstition. Youths clad in skins ran around the city with whips to chase away bad luck. They struck any woman they met a blow which was supposed to confer fertility.

These superstitious Romans presented the Pope with a petition asking for the revival of the Lupercalia. Gelasius replied quickly and with anger: "What! Is it you who accuse us of being remiss and cowardly in censuring the crimes of the Church! And who are you, I ask? Really, you are neither

Christians nor pagans, but rather men without faith or morals." Gelasius forbade all Catholics from having anything to do with the affair, and this pagan rite soon ended. He replaced the Lupercalia by the Feast of the Purification. The Feast of the Purification, kept on February 2, commemorates the Purification of the Blessed Virgin in the Temple of Jerusalem. It is also called Candlemas, from the candles which are blessed and carried in procession on that day.

In his zeal for the beauty and majesty of Divine service, Gelasius I composed many hymns, prefaces, and collects, and arranged a standard Mass book. He died on November 19, 496 A.D. Like St. Victor I and St. Miltiades – the other two African Popes – Gelasius I was canonized. As a Saint, his Feast-day is held on November 21. St. Gelasius I has been described as great, even among the saints.

For their devoted, faithful service and their deeds and piety, the Church of Rome owes much to these three African pontiffs – Saint Victor I, Saint Miltiades and Saint Gelasius I.

****

PRIMARY REFERENCES:

This work is based primarily on a 30-minute British Broadcasting Corporation program in London, broadcast on Good Friday, April 15, 1960, titled African Popes, written and compiled by Edward Scobie, author of this work. The program was produced by the late J.M.G. (Tom) Adams, former Prime Minister of Barbados.

OTHER REFERENCES:

Brusher, Joseph S. *Popes through the Ages.*
(New Jersey: Princeton. 1959)

Holtzclaw, Robert Fulton, *The Saints Go Marching In*
(Keeble Press Inc, 1980)

New Catholic Encyclopedia, Vols. VI, IX, XIV (McGraw-Hill 1967)

Ottley, Roi. *No Green Pastures* (London: John Murray 1952)

CHAPTER THREE

The Moors And Portugal's Global Expansion

For all the negroes or black Moors are descendants of Cush, the son of Ham, who was the son of Noah. But whatever difference there is between the negroes and the tawny Moors, it is a fact that they are all of the same ancestry.

Leo Africanus, A Geographical History of Africa, 1600

The ancestry to which Leo Africanus was referring is African. European scholars in the past five hundred years have been deliberately dishonest in their writings about Africa. There are innumerable instances, much too numerous to catalogue in this work of this dishonesty. However, we cannot ignore the fact that certain western scholars have claimed that the Moors belonged to every other race except African. As a result much confusion has been spread around the word "Moor."

This study is not intended to prolong the discussion about who the Moors were or who they were not. Scholars who are not blinded by the fog of racism are of one voice that all Moors were africoid in origin, even those marauding Arabs who crossed the desert sands of Arabia and swept down with their Islamic fervor upon northern regions of Africa before crossing the Sahara and moving further southward. All this while miscegenation was taking place, producing peoples of

**THE ACTOR ALDRIDGE AS THE MOOR
OTHELLO**

African descent who were all shades, from jet black to very near white. Dr. Chancellor Williams hits the nail on the head, once and for all, when he asks and answers the question:

> Now, again, just who were the Moors? The answer is very easy. The original Moors, like the original Egyptians, were Black Africans. As amalgamation became more and more widespread, only the Berbers, Arabs and coloureds in the Moroccan territories were called Moors, while the darkest and black skinned Africans were called "Black-a-Moors". Eventually, "black" was dropped from "Blackamoor". In North Africa – and Morocco – in particular all Muslim Arabs, mixed breeds and Berbers are readily regarded as Moors. The African Blacks, having had even this name taken from them, must contend for recognition as Moors.

Dr. J. C. DeGraft-Johnson, M.A., B. Com, Ph.D, in his study, African Glory (The Story of Vanished Negro Civilization), states categorically that:

> It was because the conquering army in Spain was largely made up of Africans from Morocco that we hear such phrases as "the Moorish invasion of Spain", and why Shakespeare's hero Othello is a Moor, and why the word "blackamoor" exists in the English language, a word which leaves no doubt as to the colour of the army of occupation in Spain and Portugal.

The term "Arabic," contends Dr. DeGraft-Johnson, must be understood in a cultural rather than a racial sense, "for the Arabs did not believe in any Herrenvolk theory and freely intermarried with those they conquered." Their conquest of North Africa, however, was no walkover except perhaps Egypt, where the Arabs were looked upon as deliverers from the oppressive rule of Byzantium. The fierce resistance mounted by Kuseila of Mauritania, and by his relative Kahina, projected the African mood at that period. In fact, so fierce and determined were the African counter-attacks that an Arab governor once saw fit to observe that the conquest of Africa was impossible.

Scarcely had a Berber tribe been exterminated when another would take its place. Nevertheless, upon conquest, Africans appear to have been converted to the Mohammedan faith particularly through the system of intermarriage that was practiced on an extensive scale by the Arabs. Among the African leaders converted to the Islamic faith during the invasion of Morocco was the great general known as Tarik. Describing Tarik and his army, who captured Spain, chroniclers of the time made note that these Moors were "a black or dark people, some being very black."

The conquest of Spain has been described by Dr. DeGraft-Johnson as an African conquest. Like other historians before and after him he made it clear that the conquerors were Mohammedan Africans, not Arabs, "who had laid low the Gothic Kingdom of Spain." The Arab quotient of this conquest was added by Professor C. P. Groves in his book *The Planting of Christianity in Africa* when he stated that the Arab leader Musa ibn Nusair "apparently taken by surprise at the speed of events, hastened across with an army the following year and completed the conquest, thus associating Arab arms with the final victory."

This statement that the Arab leader Musa ibn Nusair had been taken by surprise by Tarik's invasion of Spain the previous year (711 A.D.) needs some clarification. It was Musa ibn Nusair who, after having invaded Morocco, gave Tarik the rank of general and left him in charge of Tangiers, which also made him governor of Mauritania. So when the African general decided that he intended crossing the straits to survey and examine the possibilities for an invasion he accordingly informed Musa ibn Nusair of his intentions. He carried out these intentions under his own leadership without the presence of Musa ibn Nusair. In 711, accompanied by 100 horses and 400 soldiers, General Tarik crossed over into Spain on this exploratory mission. He made landfall near the Spanish town of Algeciras and finding the country with virtually little or no defense, he ravaged the neighboring towns with his small army returning to Africa laden with spoils. It was at this stage that Tarik gave an account of his mission to Musa ibn Nusair and later that same year he set sail again for Spain, this time in command of an army of 7,000 Africans.

The story of this second invasion of the Iberian Peninsula by African and Arab warriors is legendary. DeGraft-Johnson called it "an African conquest." Basil Davidson, who has been recognized as the most distinguished of historians, declared that there were no lands at that time (the eighth century) "more admired by its neighbors, or more comfortable to live in, than a rich African kingdom which took shape in Spain." It is good to observe here that Basil Davidson did not resort to the words "Arab kingdom" but that does not mean that Arab arms did not take part in the final victory.

It was this Moorish invasion under the leadership of the African General Tarik, which spurred the first great wave of miscegenation. In less than three years the Moors had conquered the entire Iberian Peninsula. The color of the conquering soldiers was described vividly by a European scholar who sympathized with Christian Spain:

> The reins of their (Moors) horses were as fire, their faces black as pitch, their eyes shone like burning candles, their horses were swift as leopards and the riders fiercer than a wolf in the sheepfold at night. The noble Goths were broken in an hour, quicker than tongue can tell. Oh, luckless Spain!

ALESSANDRO DEI MEDICI
First Duke of France known as
Alessandro The Moor

Other writers were not of the opinion that the conquest of Spain and Portugal was a disaster. The Whites in those Iberian countries were not viewed in a favorable light:

> They are nearer animals than men. They are by nature unthinking and their manners crude. Their bellies protrude; their color is white and their hair is long. In sharpness and delicacy of spirit and in intellectual perspicacity they are nil. Ignorance, lack of reasoning power and boorishness are common among them.

The Moors had a particularly low opinion of these Whites. They had beaten them often on the battlefield and with inferior numbers. Even the Europeans in other countries of this continent were looked upon with disdain for their low intelligence and base ways of life. Modern White historians agree with Moorish writer Michaud in his *History of the Crusades* when he describes the Prussians of the thirteenth century as being just a few stages above savagery. The palaces of the then-rulers of Germany, France and England were, when compared with those of the Moorish rulers of Spain and Portugal, "scarcely better than the stables" of the Moors. The education of the Moors was at such a high level that their scholars of Toledo, Cordova and Seville were producing treatises on spherical trigonometry, when the mathematical syllabus of the University of Oxford stopped abruptly at the fifth proposition of the book of Euclid. It was this superior intellect of the Moors which caused Stanley Lane-Poole in his famous *The Story of the Moors in Spain* to note: "Whatever makes a kingdom great, whatever tends to refinement and civilization was found in Moorish Spain."

The same degree of intellect and learning was brought by the Moorish conquerors of the Iberian Peninsula to Portugal. Like Spain, that country was to be culturally influenced by the Moors. Its association with Africa dates as far back as the fourth and fifth centuries when Africans arrived in southern Europe.

But it was in 711 A.D. that they marched in as conquerors under the command of Tarik. To reinforce what has been said earlier, these Moors, as the early writers chronicled, were "a black or dark people, some being very black."

After the invasion of 711 came other waves of Moors, even darker. It was this occupation of Portugal that accounts for the fact that even noble families had absorbed the blood of the Moor. From that time onwards, racial mixing in Portugal, as in Spain and elsewhere in Europe that came under the influence of Moors, took place on a large scale. That is why historians claim that "Portugal is in reality a Negroid land," and that when Napoleon explained that "Africa began at the Pyrenees," he meant every word that he uttered. Even the world-famed Fatima shrine in Portugal, where Catholic pilgrims from all over the world go in search of miracle cures for their afflictions, owes its origin to the Moors. The story goes that a Portuguese nobleman was so saddened by the death of his wife, a young Moorish beauty whom he had married after her conversion to the Christian faith, that he gave up his title and fortune and entered the monastery. His wife was buried on a high plateau called Sierra de Aire. It is from there that the name of Fatima is derived.

The Moors ruled and occupied Lisbon and the rest of the country until well into the twelfth century. They were finally defeated and driven out by the forces of King Alfonso Henriques, who was aided by English and Flemish crusaders. The scene of this battle was the Castelo de Sao Jorge (the Castle of St. George). Today, it still stands, overlooking the city of "Lashbuna" – as the Moors named Lisbon.

The defeat of the Moors did not put an end to their influence on Portugal. The African (Moorish) presence can be seen everywhere in Portugal, in the architecture of many of the buildings. They still retain their Moorish, design like the Praca De Toiros, the Bull Ring in Lisbon. A walk through Alfama – the oldest quarter in Lisbon, with its fifteenth-century houses, narrow, winding streets – dates back to the time when it was the last settlement of the Moors. Fado singers abound in all corners and bistros of Alfama. Their songs and rhythms owe much to the influence of the Moorish musicians centuries ago. Even the fishing boats on the beaches of Cascais show marked African traces. Called the rabelos, these boats with their large red or white sails, which also ply on the Douro River to fetch wine from the upper valleys, are reminiscent of the transport boats of Lagos in Nigeria.

A deeper examination of Portugal within the time frame of the Moorish invasion and occupation reveals a constant intermingling of White and Moor. Historians claimed that the mingling of the races in Portugal, as with Spain, "had much to do with the later high civilization reached by the Moors." The African element was more predominant in Portugal than it was in Spain, some historians contend. The noble families in Portugal and in Spain as well, who had absorbed the blood of the Moor were innumerable. Even some of the knights, who distinguished themselves in the wars of conquest, had such blood. Of the Count of Coimbra, Don Sesnado, the chronicles tell us that he was of mixed blood, of Christian and Moor, and that he was a vizier among the Saracens. Another of mixed blood, Dom Fifes Serrasim, became a member of the Christian nobility by marrying a Mendes de Braganza.

Many European historians who constantly project bias scholarship in their writings of Africa and Africans, persist in denying the tremendous cultural and genetic influence, that the Moors (Africans) had on the countries of the Iberian Peninsula, particularly Portugal and Spain. One scholar, Gandia, stated bluntly:

As to the mixture of Moors and the other inhabitants

of the Iberian Peninsula it is useless to deny its occurrence. Without going into the social life of the Christians and Moslems, it may be mentioned in passing that the son of Musa married the widow of King Roderick and that the royal family of Witza united with the Moors of the purest stock.

In order to get a clearer picture of what this marriage of the son of Musa, signified in terms of unifying "with the Moors of the purest stock," it is necessary to trace the lineage of "the son of Musa" and Musa himself. To give his full name, Musa ibn Nusair was the African-Arab Governor of Morocco whom Count Julien, the Governor of Cueta on the northern tip of Morocco, contacted in 709 A.D. and encouraged to invade Spain. In June, 712, Musa ibn Nusair crossed the straits with 18,000 troops, mostly Berbers, to support Tarik against a possible strike-back by King Roderick. Musa captured Carmona, Medina, Sidonia, and Ceremona while his son, Abd al Aziz, took Seville, Niebla and Beja. After this conquest of Spain, Musa put his three sons in charge of the armies in Spain and North Africa: Abd al Aziz in Spain, and the other two in Morocco and Algeria and Tunisia.

Although marriage and mixture took place on an extensive scale in Spain and Portugal between White and Moor, the union of Egilona, widow of King Roderick, and Abd al Aziz, eventually led to the assassination of the latter in 716 as a result of the bitter resentment that the marriage caused among Muslims. Aziz was succeeded as commander of the army in Spain by his cousin, Ayyub ibn Habib, who was eventually replaced by al-Hurr ibn Abdurrahman. At this stage of succession, Muslim rulers were instrumental in extending their rule from Spain and Portugal to many areas in France. In 717 and 719, Hurr crossed the treacherous passes of the Pyrenees and entered France. Unrest in Spain prevented him from gaining any strong foothold in France. It was not until 729 that another Moorish ruler, Haytham ibn Ubayad, was successful in capturing Lyon, Macon and Chalons sur Saone in France. Beaune and Autun were also under the control of the Berbers; it was a Berber leader named Uthman ibn Abu-Nisah, known sometimes as Munuza, who governed not only Spain but parts of France as well. Munuza established excellent relationships with the Christians of France, Spain and Portugal, and married Lampegie, the daughter of Duke Eudes of Aquitaine.

This period of Moorish rule between 719 and 729 was rife with intrigue and treachery. When al-Hurr ibn Abdurrahman was replaced by ab-Samh ibn Malik, the latter transferred the Spanish capital from Seville to Cordoba. He completely reorganized the finances of the country and system of taxation by carrying out several public works and putting into operation an extensive survey of the land. He died in May 721 and was replaced by Abdurrahman ibn Abdullah, who was quickly deposed in favor of Yahya ibn Salmah. In rapid succession two other Muslim rulers took control but were finally ousted; once again Abdurrahman ibn Abdullah gained office.

Abdullah proved to be a strong ruler. Under his leadership, the rival factions in the Empire became reconciled, but he was challenged by Munuza. Because of that challenge, Abdullah set about the destruction of Munuza, who had entered into intrigue with his father-in-law, Duke Eudes. Abdullah finally succeeded in killing Abu-Nisah, known also as Munuza, and sending the latter's wife to Damascus, where she married the son of the Caliph, Hisham.

Abdullah then crossed the Pyrenees and delivered a crushing blow against Duke Eudes on the Garonne, sacked Bordeaux, and went across Politiers into Tours. It was at this point in 732 that Abdullah went in to battle Charles Martel. He died in that fight, and Tours marked the western limit of the Umayyad Empire. It is universally agreed that the Berbers, with

BLACK NORMAN KNIGHT AND HIS FAIR LADY

their Black blood mixed with some Arab, became a conquering people. They would have taken the whole of France had they not clashed with Charles Martel in Tours. However, they remained in Southern France until 1140, principally in the Camarque on the western Riviera, which is still known as La Petite Afrique.

In the centuries that were to follow, these same African (Moorish) conquerors civilized backward Spain and Portugal. The court of the Moorish rulers at Cordoba became the center of culture. Art, learning, refinement and elegance marked the reign of these African conquerors. Commerce flourished; mathematics, science and medicine found their way through the cultural darkness of Spain. This same cultural enlightenment was taken to Portugal by the conquering Moors of Africa. Contact with the Far East brought Spain and Portugal a real renaissance when other parts of Europe were spending a thousand years passing through the Dark Ages, which was brought about by the destruction of Rome by the barbarians.

Moorish domination extended to parts of Italy. In 846 A.D., they held the city of Rome in a state of siege while in 878 they captured Sicily from the Normans. Twenty years later the Moors took control of Southern Italy by defeating Otto II of Germany. As in Spain and Portugal, miscegenation took place on a wide scale between the Moors and the Italians who, at that time, had large infusions of Germanic blood due to the invasion of the Goths and Vandals.

As in Portugal and Spain, the blood of Africa permeated through all layers of Italian society and found its way into the leading families, including the most illustrious royal family of the times: the Medicis. Color was no bar to power and honor in Italy.

The Moors also dominated the British Isles at one point in history. The British archaeologist and writer David McRitchie

MOORS AND THEIR COAT OF ARMS

declared that the Moors dominated Scotland as late as the time of the Saxon Kings. He stated with scholarly authority:

> So late as the tenth century three of these provinces (of Scotland) were wholly black and the supreme ruler of these became for a time the, paramount king of transmarine Scotland. We see one of the

> black people– the Moors of the Romans – in the person of a King of Alban of the tenth century. History knows him as Kenneth, sometimes as Dubh and as Niger... We know as a historic fact that a Niger Val Dubh has lived and reigned over certain black divisions of our islands –and probably white divisions also – and that a race known as the "Sons of the Black" succeeded him in history.

It is no exaggeration, then, to claim that the Moors were a leading power in those six or seven centuries from the time of Tarik's conquest on the Iberian Peninsula. They dominated the Mediterranean and the North Atlantic and held power over the coasts of Western Europe and the British Isles, as has been stated earlier. But it is not for their military conquests in Europe that the Moors are remembered. It is the culture and learning that they gave to European countries at a time when there was darkness, and nothing elevating, in the arts and sciences of a country that was to falsely claim, in later centuries, to be the cradle of the civilization of the world. That this civilization was first given to them by the Africans who remained in European countries for several centuries, has stayed shrouded in perjuries, half-truths, mythologies and/or total omissions. This civilization, brought by the African Moors, needs further and deeper examination, especially as Spain and Portugal were the first countries in Europe to benefit from the enlightenment which the African warrior-scholars carried with them from across the African mainland through the Mediterranean Sea to Iberia, and to other European countries further inland. In

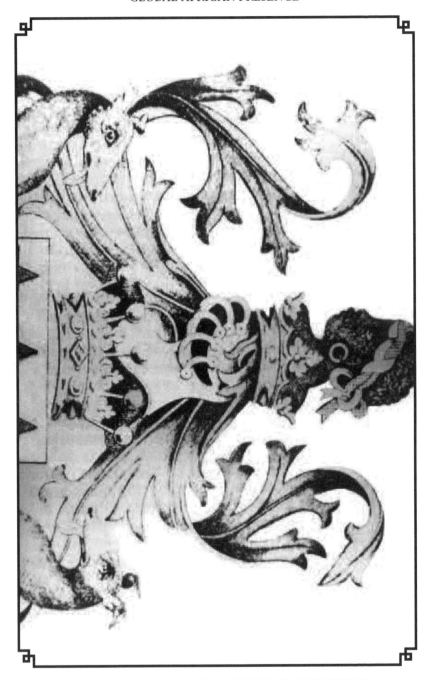

**FAMILY CREST FROM BRITAIN SHOWING
MOORISH WOMAN**

Britain, for instance, the Morris dance, England's national dance which has been performed every May Day for centuries, was originally a dance performed by the Moors. It is of African origin, and was introduced in England before William the Conqueror in 1066. Sir John Hawkins, an eighteenth-century man-of-letters and music authority in London, wrote: "It is indisputable that this dance was the invention of the Moor."

Tabourot, another authority, chronicled the same strong statement. Dr. Samuel Johnson, who compiled the first English dictionary in the middle years of the eighteenth century, defined the Morris dance as "A Moorish dance" and the invention of the Moors in England in the seventeenth century. Any kind of entertainment or masquerade was called "Mauresque," wrote Paul Nettl, "because the guise of the black man was the most important and popular, a phenomenon which points on the one hand to the significance of the black race for the aesthetic life of the whites; on the other hand, to the ancient habit of all Europeans to paint the face black on certain occasions of cult ritualism." Nettl quotes Arbeau, the French writer of the sixteenth century, who stated that often in good society he would see "a youth with blackened face" do this Morris dance. In the Italian madrigal literature of the Renaissance, says Arbeau, "real Negroes were introduced." Real African minstrels were popular entertainers in the Scottish and Tudor courts of England during the fifteenth century.

Queen Elizabeth I had one favorite African in her Tudor court. She was Luce Morgan, also known as Lucy Negro. Elizabethan history tells much about this fascinating African beauty who was sought after by gentlemen in the Inns of Court in London, titled men, including even William Shakespeare. Her association with the Bard of Avon was not only intriguing but mysterious as well. That love affair has been meticulously swept under the carpets of English history. But eventually the truth will always show itself; this one is now known to an ever-growing number of scholars. The effect that Luce Morgan had on Elizabethan England was tremendous.

In the England of the Tudor monarchs in the fifteenth century and after, such were the scenes in the various cities during the twilight of the power of the Moors in Europe. Another kind of African was making entry into Europe, this time not as conqueror, but as captive. But that is another story with tragic dimensions. Let us go back to the conquering but scholarly African Moors who peopled the Iberian Peninsula and other areas of that backward continent of Europe. They were the first to bring the benefits of civilization and scholarship to a continent sunk in the very abyss of vulgarity and barbarism.

David McRitchie produces enough evidence to prove that a race of Africans (Moors) lived in Scotland and parts of England well back into the tenth century. He writes, "Our language still retains the memory of their presence," and goes on to say that:

> In Shakespeare's time the audience at the Globe accepted the word as meaning "a black man", and either then, or later on, it became tautologically extended into "blackamoor." The common people of the country are not likely to have known much about the ultra-British "Moors," – not enough at any rate, to have made the word an everyday term for a black man. Nor can the Moors of heraldry be explained sufficiently by the theory that the founders of families bearing Moors as supporters, and Moors' heads as crests, had won their spurs in assisting the Spaniards expel their Moors. The bearing is too common among ancient coats-of-arms to admit of this explanation. And the heraldic representation of a "Moor" does not suggest Granada.

McRitchie gives the names of many of these families (Moorish) whose names are quite celebrated in English history. One of these is the aristocratic Douglas family, said to be one of the ancestors of the present royal family of Britain. A British authority, J.A. Ringrose, explains about the founder of this family:

> About the year 770 in the reign of Salvathius, King of the Scots, Donald Bane of the Western isles having invaded Scotland and routed the royal army, a man of rank and figure came seasonably with his followers to the King's assistance. He renewed the battle and obtained a complete victory over the invader. The king being anxious to see the man who had done him such signal service, he was pointed out to him by his colour, or complexion in Gaelic language – sholto-du-glash – "behold the black or swarthy coloured man" from which he obtained the name Sholto the Douglas.

McRitchie further states that the most revealing evidence of the Moorish origin of these noble families is "the thick-lipped Moors" on their coats-of-arms. Many of these families still carry the name Moore. Barry's *Encyclopedia Heraldica* notes on its pages that "Moor's head is the heraldic term for the head of a black or negro man." McRitchie contends that the racial origin of these notable families stems from the fact that there were Black peoples (Moors or Silures) domiciled in Scotland as early as the ninth and tenth centuries. Added to that, some of the bearers of the insignia of the Moor's heads are named Moore. Among the latter are the Rt. Hon. William Ponsonby Moore, Earl of Drogheda; Moore of Hancot; Moore of Moore Lodge; the Earl of Annesly; and Morrison-Bell of Otterburn. According to *Burke's Peerage*, the bible of British aristocracy, the coat-of-arms of the Marquess of Londonderry consists of "a Moor wreathed about the temples, arg. and az., holding in his exterior hand a shield of the last garnished or, charged with the sun in splendor, gold." Bearers of similar coats-of-arms are the Earl of Newburgh; Viscount Valentia, whose family is related to Annesly and whose arms bear a Moorish prince in armor; and Baron Whitburgh.

McRitchie maintains that these noble families were descendants of the Moors of the very earlier centuries who had been bred out until the Black man finally disappeared by mating with Whites only. He wrote:

> No ethnologist could detect the presence of other blood, and yet in both cases, the male descendant would bear the surname signifying "the black man..." you may see faces of a distinctly Mongolian and even of a Negroid cast in families whose pedigree may be traced for many generations without disclosing the slightest hint of extra British blood ... so far as complexion goes there can be no doubt as to the presence of a vast infusion of "coloured" blood. There are, of course, no living Britons who are as black as negroes but some are as dark as mulattoes and many darker than Chinese. To regard ourselves in the mass as a "white people" except in a comparative degree, is quite a mistake.

The families with the name of Moor, Moore, Morris, Morrison, too, and other derivatives of Moor, had Moors as their ancestors, stated McRitchie. Families with Moors in the coats-of-arms ranged from Sicily to Finland, and were also included in Britain, France, Germany, Holland, Italy, Switzerland, Poland, Denmark and Sweden. McRitchie was convinced that some African blood also mixed with Norman blood, which is the word in British "blue blood". Listed among those were the Morrices, Fitz-Morices and Mountmorrices (all variations of Moor). A noted writer on heraldry, Lower, says of these August families: "They are supposed to be of Moorish blood; their progenitors having come from Africa by way of Spain into various countries of Western Europe."

Not only did the Moors in their European conquests leave their learning, they left their culture and arts as well. Their blood, the blood of Africa, was to remain and flow in the veins of many a European, be he aristocrat or commoner. Finally, it is left now to investigate, in some detail, that culture which these Islamic sons of Africa left for the benefit of Europe; particularly Spain and, even more so, Portugal. It is this African cultural heritage that set in motion the expansion of Europe.

European expansion on a global scale can be chronicled from the last years of the fifteenth century. By the coming of the next century, the world known to western man had reached great proportions to span almost the entire earth's sphere. The explorers, Da Gama, Columbus, Cabot, Cabral, Magellan and many others, had brought Europeans to the farthest reaches of this planet, setting in motion what has been called the global epoch of European expansion.

When the reasons for this mammoth expansion in the sixteenth century are examined, certain explanations become crystal clear. To put it bluntly, it was the part Africa played in providing the learning that triggered off this expansion. The culture of North Africa, the resources of Central Africa, and equipment of Moorish science set off a spate of explorations, which culminated in the circumnavigation of the globe.

The great part played by Africa in supplying the learning, which caused the expansion to take place, has had little, if any, exposure in the writings of historians. The question was never posed as to why the Iberian countries were in the forefront of this global expansion. The British, the French, the Dutch and the Italians owned the ships that could undertake this journey. Their leaders also possessed the necessary vision for such an enterprise. Yet they did not take the lead. With respect to overseas expansion they were always trailing way behind the Iberians. One may well ask at this point, why was that so?

Put quite simply, the answer is that the outstanding factor, which set Spain and Portugal apart from their neighbors in the north, was their most valuable inheritance from Africa. The rich cultural, artistic, and scientific knowledge inherited from the Moors placed Spain and Portugal well ahead of the rest of Europe, still backward and living in the Dark Ages. More than that, the Moors (Arab and Berbers) struck the blow that completed the decay of ancient Spain and established Moorish Spain. This Spain was to herald one of the brightest chapters in the intellectual history of Medieval Europe. Portugal, too, played an equal role in bringing this about. Professor Thomas T. Hamilton of Old Dominion University made this point clearly when he stated:

> Between the middle of the eighth and the beginning of the thirteenth centuries the Arabic-speaking people (Moors) were the main bearers of the torch of civilization throughout the world, and were the medium through which ancient science was recovered, supplemented and transported through Africa, Spain and Sicily in such a way as to make the Renaissance possible.

Cordova, Seville and Toledo remained the centers of Moorish culture and science. Students from many countries of Western Europe were made welcome at the universities of these three cities. It was at Cordova that Gerbert of Aurillac gained mastery over mathematics. When he became Pope Sylvester II, this caused him to introduce the use of Arabic numerals in the Latin West. The works of Aristotle first appeared in Europe through the Moors in Spain.

The center of scientific learning remained in Toledo even though it had been reconquered by Castile in 1085. In Toledo, many converted Moors and Jews translated several mathematical, astronomical and astrological works. Included in these works was a series of astronomical tables based on the work of a group of Afro-Arabs and Jewish predecessors. These studies, known as the Toledo Tables, contained not only astronomical material but geographical information as well. Gerard of Cremona, who undertook most of this work in Toledo, translated these studies into Latin in the twelfth century.

By then Portugal and Spain were far ahead of the rest of the European countries in intellectual attachments. This advance was made possible by the proximity of Africa to Spain and what has been rightly termed "the aggressiveness of the North African Berbers". It was these people of North Africa who brought this intellectual atmosphere and the advantages of their civilization, and so put those Iberian countries at the very front and caused them, indeed, to be the pioneers of European global expansion.

The invasion of the Moors on the Iberian Peninsula in 711 was unique in certain aspects. First, a few thousand men took over the government, only to be driven out of the area by a few thousand armed men, seven centuries later. In between those hundreds of years, the majority of the populations of both Spain and Portugal were left comparatively undisturbed. Professor Hamilton gives a very revealing account of the situation in Spain and Portugal during these seven hundred-plus years:

> The overwhelming majority of the people under the caliphs were the same people whose descendants were to discover the world for Spain and Portugal. The Christian rulers displaced the political and religious power of the Moslem rulers. The artists, scientists, writers and ordinary people were the holdovers connecting the two civilizations. The Mozarabs who took the lead in economic and cultural life of the new Spain were not Arabs, but rather were African Berbers, who, as time went by, were assimilated into the basic Iberian stock.

Furthermore, when the Christian princes regained the peninsula, the old civilization was not destroyed. Religious art, of course, was influenced adversely, but the actual scientific achievements were retained, and Toledo became a great translation center under the Castilians. While the rural districts continued their futile feudalism as they had both before and during the Moslem rule, the cities continued to bloom, thanks to the vitalizing influence of the Mozarabs and the Jews.

It was into this intellectually advanced civilization in 1394 that Prince Henry the Navigator was born. By that time and in the following century, Portugal was judged to possess a culture that had no equal north of the Pyrenees. This culture had traveled with the African Moors and came into full blossom mostly in Spain; but during the occupation, Portugal was an integral part of the Cordovan Caliphate. Eminent scholars have agreed that the talents of the Portuguese in geography and navigation have come out of this rich African heritage. In fact, long before the birth of Prince Henry, the Spanish and African Moors had excelled in these sciences. Hamilton explains why the Moors held pre-eminence in terrestrial mathematics, which is essential in the science of navigation, claiming that it could be traced to their religion:

> Their faith required them to pray at a specified time each day in the exact direction of Mecca. In order for the devout moslem to accomplish this it was necessary for him to have the geographical coordinates of his location, just as a mariner must have his position. Thus did geodesy become an exact science in the world of Islam.

The Afro-Iberian Moors were responsible for almost all the geographical lore which the Europeans, primarily the Portuguese and Spanish, used in their global expansion. This knowledge was divided into three main categories: the systemic geographers and encyclopedists, who incorporated the lore of the ancients with the discoveries of their contemporaries; the astronomers and geodesists, who set out the groundwork for navigation and cartography; and, lastly, the travelers and collectors of travel accounts, thus providing the descriptions of the world. Through religion and trade, the Muslim world placed great stake on travel; and more than any other peoples during those early centuries, they traveled the length and breadth of the known world, by foot, camel, donkey and cows, Muslims entered remote lands. Of the travel accounts available at that time was the narrative of Ibn Battutah, called the most widely traveled scholar of the Middle Ages. In the fourteenth century he traversed the entire span of Muslim countries, from China to Guinea.

Ibn Hawkel, another Moorish writer who wrote during that time, said that slaves, ivory and gold dust were important items in the Mediterranean trade. Until the advent of the Moslem writers, written information about Africa was very scant indeed. It was these scribes who used information about Africa and travel to its interior to reach European ears, especially the people of Iberia and Sicily. One such traveler with whose writings Prince Henry was very familiar was Ibn Battutah. In the year 1352, Battutah penetrated the interior of Africa and produced the most complete portrait of the African peoples up to that time. He meticulously kept a chronological narrative of his travels and noted how very well he got on with the local rulers in the areas that he visited. He made mention on several occasions of having received gifts of gold dust from the African monarchs. This knowledge proved to be of great value not only to Prince Henry, but to other Iberian explorers who were to claim vast landmasses for Portugal and Spain.

It was in the fifteenth century that the precious metals in Europe had been drastically depleted due to the demands of enormous foreign trade and the very costly wars that had been fought and were still taking place. During that period, due to the limitation of camel travel, bulky goods from the west could not stand the heavy cost of being carried to the East. The valuable goods from India, China and the Spice Islands, which were taken overland, had to be paid in gold and silver. In the past, Europe could depend on her own mines, but with the depletion due to the costliness of her wars, her merchants traded with Barbary using gold taken from Guinea. Consequently, it was not surprising that with her gold shortage, yet still requiring that precious commodity, Europe would turn to Africa as an untapped source of supply. It was this shortage of gold and other precious metal in Europe that prompted their penetration of Saharan Africa.

Prince Henry and all his scholarly associates had great knowledge of this information about the science of the Afro-Iberian Moors. The Portuguese explorers became well aware that it would be the riches of Africa that would supply the vast amounts of gold needed by the crown of Portugal. It was these two factors that were the primary objectives for the Portuguese exploration of the lands of Africa and the Indies. These motives remained of paramount importance until the death of Prince Henry in 1460, and afterward. Hamilton concluded that, "The background of the African Moor and the lure of African gold broke the fetters that bound the European to Europe." Much praise was heaped on the royal head of Prince Henry for the great part he played in the early Portuguese explorations. He has even been immortalized in the volumes of history as "Prince Henry the Navigator." What remains minimized and almost unwritten in the pages of the history of Europe and its global expansion is the very vital role that the Moors played. For without their scholarly writings and their extensive mastery of the sciences of navigation, cartography, astronomy and mathematics, the voyages of the Portuguese and Spanish would not have taken place. Yet Prince Henry has reaped all the glory. In talking about this, Hamilton throws true light on this legend and gives honor where honor is due:

> Prince Henry...had swept away from the minds of even the legends of the unearthly terrors which had hitherto precluded voyages into the unknown. He had proved the feasibility of Atlantic travel and had provided and perfected the ships and instruments to reduce the actual dangers to be encountered.

> Diaz, Columbus, DaGama, Cabral, Vespucci and Magellan were fruit of the tree planted by Prince Henry. The chains were broken by the lore and lure of Africa. Africa not only influenced European expansion; it determined it.

The influence of the Moors ranged further afield in Europe and has also been ignored by European writers after the Africans were eventually driven back to Africa. Some honest historians have deplored this behavior and sought to include the whole story of the conquest of Europe by the Moors in their annals. One such scholar was John William Draper, M.D. LL.D, Professor of Chemistry and Physiology at the University of New York in latter years of the nineteenth century. In his classic work *History of the Intellectual Development Europe*, Draper stated clearly:

> I have to deplore the systematic manner in which the literature of Europe has contrived to put out of sight our scientific obligations to the Mohammedans. Surely they cannot be much longer hidden. Injustice founded on religious rancor and national conceit cannot be perpetrated forever.

The list of Moorish achievement is endless. Draper asks:

> What should the modern astronomer say when, remembering the contemporary barbarism of Europe, he finds the Arab Abdul Hasson speaking

of tubes, to the extremities of which ocular and object diopters, perhaps sights, were attached, as used at Meragha? What when he reads of the attempts of Abderrhman Sufi at improving the photometry of the stars? Are the astronomical tables of Ebn Junis (A.D. 1008) called the Hakemite tables, or the Ilkanic tables of Nasser Eddin Tasi, constructed at the great observatory just mentioned, Meragha, near Tauris, A.D. 1259, or the measurement of time by pendulum oscillations, and the methods of correcting astronomical tables by systematic observations – are such things worthless indications of the mental state? The Arab (Moor) has left his intellectual impress on Europe, as, long before, Christendom will have to confess; he has indelibly written it on the heavens, as anyone may see who reads the names of the stars on a common celestial globe.

In other fields of development, the Moors left Portugal and Spain far ahead of the rest of Europe. They set an example of skillful agriculture, cultivating plants, introducing many new ones; breeding cattle and sheep and fine horses. To them Europe owes the introduction of products like rice, sugar, cotton; and all the fine garden and orchard fruits, together with many less important plants such as spinach and saffron. The Moors brought the culture of silk to Europe, and they gave to Xeres and Malaga their knowledge of winemaking (something for which the two Iberian countries have earned a worldwide reputation). But the story does not end here. The Moorish conquerors introduced the Egyptian system of irrigation by floodgates, wheels and pumps. They also promoted many vital branches of industry and improved the manufacture of textiles, fabrics, earthenware, iron, steel; the Toledo sword blades were valued everywhere for their power. Upon expulsion from Spain and Portugal, the Moors carried the manufacture of a kind of leather, in which they were acknowledged to excel, to Morocco. It is known throughout the world for its excellence as Moroccan leather.

The Moors also introduced inventions of a more ominous nature – gunpowder and artillery. The cannons they used appear to have been forged from wrought iron. But of more value to Portugal and Spain was the introduction of the mariner's compass, something that aided the explorers of Iberia to gain control of vast expanses of the New World.

The manufacture of the cannons was made possible by gunpowder brought by the Moors; and with their ships using lateen sails, astrolabes and nautical compasses, all the inventions of the Afro-Arab Moors; the Portuguese and Spanish set sail to rob the resources of others. In the words of Ghanaian scholar, Samuel Kennedy Yeboah, "The Europeans unleashed a concerted and, in some cases, genocidal (e.g. the aborigines and some of the Amerindians) onslaught against the rest of the world."

What were Spain and Portugal like when the illustrious Moors were finally driven off from these Iberian lands? They left farming, the arts, sciences; beautiful cities with magnificent buildings, gardens, streets and a culture and civilization far surpassing that of the rest of Europe. The city of Cordova, under their administration, at its highest point of posterity had more than 200,000 houses and over a million inhabitants. At night one could walk through it in a straight line for ten miles by the light of the public lamps. Seven hundred years after this time there was not as much as one public lamp in London. The streets of Cordova were solidly paved. In Paris, centuries later whoever walked over his threshold on a rainy day would be covered in mud right up to his ankles. Other Iberian cities like Grenada, Seville, Toledo, and Lisbon considered themselves rivals in magnificence with Cordova. The palaces of the Khalifs were handsomely decorated.

But this beauty, this culture, this civilization, was not to last very long under the barbarous handling by the Christians of Aragon, Castile and Portugal. They defiled the holy name of religion with its intrigues, its bloodshed, its oppression of human thought, and its hatred of intellectual advancement. This condition of destruction and decay is painstakingly described in the words of Stanley-Lane Poole in his classic *The Story of the Moors in Spain*:

> In 1492 the last bulwark of the Moors gave way before the crusades of Ferdinand and Isabella, and with Granada fell all Spain's greatness. For a brief while, indeed, the reflection of the Moorish splendor cast a borrowed light on the history of the land that it had once warmed with its sunny radiance...
>
> Then followed the abomination of desolation, the rule of the Inquisition, and the blackness of darkness in which Spain had been plunged ever since... and beggars, friars, and bandits took the place of scholars, merchants, and knights. So low fell Spain when she had driven away the Moors. Such is the melancholy contrast offered by her history.

The Moorish contact with Portugal was to have more dire consequences for Africa and African peoples. To begin with, the effects of Muslim civilization on Europe, particularly Portugal, were closely linked to the effort to reconstruct the processes by which the African past was extracted from European consciousness. There is little doubt that one of the greatest ironies of this history was the founding of the Portuguese state and the elite class that ran it. The "Age of Discovery," which Portugal used the learnings of Prince Henry that were extracted and copied from Muslim scholarship, marks the beginning of the modern era in European development. This expansion of the Portuguese into Africa and the New World set in motion the encounters between the peoples of the European peninsula and the African peoples. This was to lead into the Atlantic Slave Trade and Slavery, two of the greatest disasters that Africans suffered, in Africa. The celebrated figures of Vasco de Gama, Alfonso de Albuquerque, Ferdinand Magellan, and others; the works of Gil Vincente and Camoens – have all been the elements that have motivated the creation and recreation of the origins of Portugal. Without the knowledge, intellect, learning and artistic brilliance of the African Moors this Renaissance in Portugal would have never – and I repeat never–come about.

This is a condition or reality that relates not only to Portugal, and Spain, but the rest of the latecomers of Europe, as well. Eurocentric scholarship cannot come to grips with this fact of history and therein lies its tragedy. It is absolutely no exaggeration to state categorically that Islam had provided for not only Portugal and Spain, but for the rest of emerging Europe a powerful, economic, scientific, artistic, political impulse; an impulse that led to European domination of the world. Eurocentric scholars boast that the Renaissance aroused Europe from its Dark Age slumber. They shy away from the truth, the total truth that but for Muslim knowledge this awakening would never have come about and certainly not at the time that it did.

It is lamentable that the European foray into Africa and other lands across the seas was initiated by Portugal using the knowledge gained from Africans in order to conquer, colonize, rape, exploit, oppress, maim and murder other Africans they had captured and chained in the prison plantations of slavery. The Moors themselves, who were banished from Portugal and Spain, suffered the same horrible fate that their descendants were to endure.

How were the Moors recompensed for their phenomenal contribution in civilizing Spain, Portugal and other areas of a Europe steeped in barbarism and darkness? The nineteenth-century English scholar, Stanley Lane-Poole, paints a picture of European savagery of the lowest form in their genocide of the Moors. 50,000 of them were brutally murdered on the famous Day of All Saints, 1570, when the honor of the apostles and the martyrs of Christendom was celebrated by the virtual martyrdom of these Moors. No less than three million Moors were banished by the first decade of the seventeenth century. To use the words of the Franciscan priest Bartholomew de Las Casas during the Columbian era, when these dastardly deeds were being perpetrated on the Moors, "Moloch must have been in the skies."

Spain and Portugal did not escape retribution. Where once wit and learning flourished, a general stagnation and degradation had fallen on their people and lands. Historians are agreed that they deserved their humiliation. Such is the terrible price that Spain and Portugal had to pay for their treatment of the Moors. As Lane-Poole concluded: "They did not understand that they had killed their golden goose".

REFERENCES:

Barashangoo, Ishakamusa, Rev. *African People and European Holidays: A Mental Genocide.* (Washington, DC: IV Dynasty Publishing Co., 1983)

Bennett, Norman R. *Africa and Europe,* (New York: Africana Publishing Co., 1975)

Bovill, E.W., *The Golden Trade of the Moors,* (London: Oxford University Press, 1970)

Cox, George 0., *African Empires and Civilizations,* (New York: African Heritage Studies Publishers, 1974)

Davidson, Basil, *Discovering Our African Heritage* (Massachusetts: Ginn & Co., 1971)

Debrunner, Hans Werner, *Presence and Prestige: Africans in Europe* (Switzerland: Basler Afrika Bibliographies, 1979)

DeGraft Johnson, J.C., *African Glory* (Toronto: George J. McLeod Ltd, 1954)

Draper, John William, *History of the Intellectual Development of Europe, Vol. 11.*(London: Bell and Dalby, 1864)

Hamilton, T., "The African Heritage in European Expansion," *Journal of Ethnic Studies* (Hampton, Virginia: Hampton Institute, September 1976)

Jackson, John G., *Introduction to African Civilization* (New York: University Books,1970)

Jackson, John G., *Man, God and Civilization* (New York: University Books, 1972)

Jackson, John G., *Ages of Gold and Silver* (American Atheist Press, Texas, 1990)

Karenga, Maulana, *Introduction to Black Studies*, California: (Kowaida Publications, 1982)

Lane-Poole, Stanley, *The Story of the Moors in Spain* (Baltimore: Black Classic Press,1990)

Livermore, H.V., *The Origins of Spain and Portugal* (London,1971)

McRitchie, David, *Ancient and Modern Britons*, Vol. I. (London, 1884)

Read, Ian, *The Moors in Spain and Portugal* (New Jersey: Rowman and Littlefield, 1974)

Robinson, Cedric I., *Black Marxism*
(London: Zed Press, 1983)

Rogers, J. A., *Nature Knows No Color-Line* (New York, 1952)

Rogers, J. A., *Sex and Race, Vol. I.* (New York, 1940)

Rogers, 1. A., *World's Great Men of Color, Vol. I.*
(New York, 1947)

Scobie, Edward, *Africa in Portugal, Flamingo*
(London: February, 1962)

Scott, S.P., *History of the Moorish Empire in Europe*
(London: J. P. Lippincott, 1904)

Townson, Duncan, *Muslim Spain*
(Lerner Publications Co., 1979)

Williams, Chancellor, *The Destruction of Black Civilization*
(Chicago: Third World Press, 1976)

Windsor, Rudolph R., *From Babylon to Timbuktu* (New York:
Exposition Press, 1969)

Woodson, Carter Goodwin, *African Heroes and Heroines*
(Washington, DC: Associated Publishers, 1939)

CHAPTER FOUR

The African Presence In Shakespearean Literature

William Shakespeare dealt with Africans in his writings in a manner that showed he had a far deeper and more personal understanding of them than most Renaissance scribes, particularly the Elizabethan ones. Like others of his time, his vision of the African, primarily in his earlier works, bore signs of the stereotype. Nevertheless, in his later works, he began to move away from that interpretation. The following works illustrate that claim: *Titus Andronicus* (circa 1590), *Dark Lady of the Sonnets* (written around 1597 and 1598) and *Othello* (1604). Reference will be made to other Shakespearean works, like *Love's Labour's Lost*, *Troilus and Cressida*, and *The Two Gentlemen of Verona*.

First of all, we need to examine the prevailing view of Africa and Africans at that time and the factors that created it. Shakespearean scholars seemed to be in accord that it was the publication of two books in London in 1555 that gave Englishmen notions of Africa. The first, William Waterman's "*The Fardle of Factions*," was praised as the supreme authority. It recounts the old legends about the wonders of Africa. The second book, published in 1555, was Richard Eden's translation of Peter Martyr's *The Decades of the New World*. It contains the very first published accounts of the first two English voyages down the west coast of Africa to Guinea. Dr. Eldred Jones, recognized authority, stated that these two volumes were the primary sources of Englishmen's knowledge of Africa in the sixteenth century, which told of the tales of the ancients as popularized by translations, and the contemporary accounts of sailors who had themselves seen Africa. Even the contemporary accounts were not free from the medieval fantasies and mythologies that persisted in the minds of Europeans, like explorers and men of letters. The importance of the first book mentioned, *The Fardle of Factions*, was not to bring forward new knowledge of the world, but to give added currency to the old stories of Africa that were shot through and through with the fictions of minds coming straight out of the dark ages of Europe.

There were two other books, which later on in the sixteenth century were to influence the thinking of Englishmen about Africa. Richard Hakluyt's, *The Principal Navigations* in 1589 was most impressive in that respect. Its importance far exceeded the author's primary aim, which was to put on record the "notable enterprises by sea," intended to counter the charges of "sluggish security and continual neglect" of such enterprises which were repeatedly being flung at the English by continental scholars. Hakluyt produced one of the classics of the English language. His pages gave to the dramatists at the time a veritable gold mine of plot and character. It is little wonder that the dramatists used North Africa – commonly called Barbary – as the venue of their plays, while very often creating their characters as though they came from further south, thus combining the dramatic effectiveness of the African's Blackness with the excitement and conflicts of the North African scene.

Information of the African coastline and of the coastal peoples was growing in sixteenth century England, but about the interior precious little was known. It was all conjecture based on the fables of old. As Eldred Jones observed: "Nothing had yet been published about the area to compete with the fantasies of Pliny and Herodotus." The most reliable and authoritative material on the interior of Africa was contained in John Leo Africanus' book, *The History and Description of Africa,* translated and published in English in the year 1600. It is known for certain that Robert Greene and Ben Johnson, among the playwrights of the time, knew the book. There is also evidence to support the belief that Shakespeare and John Webster were also aware of it. In fact, there is strong circumstantial evidence to prove that Shakespeare not only used Leo Africanus' information on the character of Moors in creating the character of Othello, but there is also the claim that the suggestions for Othello's "history" come from the life of Africanus himself, as given in John Pory's introduction. There is no doubt that the correspondence between Leo Africanus' career and Othello's account of himself are striking. Africanus had not been royally born but, according to John Pory, "his parentage seemeth not to have been ignoble," and his intercourse had been mainly in the courts of princes. Like Othello he had been a traveler, had been captured and sold into slavery, and had been converted to Christianity. However, what links Leo Africanus and Othello very securely together were the indictments given by both of them against their European counterparts. This was a point put forward by the young scholar, Rosalind Johnson, in a thesis in which she illustrates parallels between Othello and Leo Africanus.

There are many such close similarities, but the most significant one that Rosalind Johnson, and a few others, have noted concerns Othello's "silk handkerchief." Miss Johnson wrote:

> Leo boasts of how "mulberrie trees" were grown in the towne of Cannis Metgara, for the "breeding of silkworms". The natives of that city were known to be "great merchants of silke". Notice that as in Shakespeare's Othello, a connection is made between the mulberry tree and silk.

> In Shakespeare's play, Othello's silken handkerchief bearing an embroidered African mulberry design

is his first gift to his wife Desdemona, and serves as a very symbolic item that helps propel the action of the tragedy.

So far, only written works that seemed to have influenced Shakespeare and other Elizabethan writers have been discussed. But there was a more important influence, particularly on William Shakespeare: personal contact with Africans, particularly Lucy Negro. This dramatic spectacle will explain the identity of Lucy Negro:

> The Gray's Inn Revels were different that Christmas of 1594. But the idea was still the same: entertainments to parody the affairs and ceremonies of the English court. The Revels would start on Halloween and last until Candlemass. A Prince of Purpool was installed on December 20th, He was two characters in one – Purpool and the Lord of Misrule. By the 28th there were so many spectators that Gray's Inn Hall became too packed for anyone to enter. That evening the actors put on *The Comedy of Errors*. Six days later the Revels were in full swing. Among those present were Lord Burleigh, the Earl of Essex, the Lord Keeper, Sir Robert Cecil and the Earls of Shrewsbury, Cumberland, Northumberland, and Southampton. The amusements began with a symbolic piece of the restoration of amity between Graius and Templarius. After that the Prince of Purpool held court. To pay homage to him came the Abbess of Clerkenwell, holder of the Nunnery and Lands and Privileges of Clerkenwell, "with a choir of Nuns, with burning lamps, to chaunt Placebo to the gentlemen of the Prince's Privy Chamber, on the Day of His Excellency's Coronation."
>
> It was the Abbess who made the difference in that year's Revels. For she was not a lady of court but a courtesan from Clerkenwell. She was tall,

statuesque, and haughty. Her name was Lucy Negro and she was in fact Black and an African. This Lucy Negro was not the only Black courtesan around Clerkenwell. There were several in the district at the time especially around "The Swan, a Dane's beershop in Turnbull Street." Here, fashionable young gentlemen of the Inns of Court used to frolic. Dr. George Bagshawe Harrison, authority on Shakespeare, claims that the Bard of Avon fell in love with Lucy Negro, the most famous courtesan of them all, only to lose her later on to the Earl of Southampton. Dr. Harrison makes a further more startling statement about Lucy Negro and Shakespeare's Dark Lady of the Sonnets.

Dr. Leslie Hotson, a man of brilliant and unorthodox scholarship and an expert on Shakespeare, throws further light on Lucy Negro after exhaustive research:

> We arrive at a beautiful harlot, Black as hell, notorious in 1588 or 1589, named Lucy or Luce... This at once takes our mind five or six years onwards to the Gesta Grayorum – the chronicle of Henry Prince of Purpoole's reign in 1594-95, and to the unsavory list of the Prince's feodaries, in which we read that a bawd named Lucy Negro "Abbess de Clerkenwell, holdeth the nunnery of Clerkenwell..."

> By this time, then, some five or six years after the Sonnets, Black Lucy or Luce has set up as the "madam" of a house in Clerkenwell. Her name was Morgan... I have been at some pains to collect facts and reports about Luce Morgan. My reward is the discovery of a series of documents indicating that some years before she charmed Shakespeare she had first charmed Queen Elizabeth.

It was quite common for Africans to take part in masques and pageants during that time – like the one called *The Masque of Blackness*, a pageant of Ethiopia staged by Ben Jonson in 1605 in which Queen Anne, wife of James I, played, and for which the ladies of the Court Blackened their faces.

In Shakespeare's lifetime and after, Blacks were very much in evidence in a particular show – London's colorful Lord Mayor's Show. One Black, known as "King of the Moors," mounted on a "lion" and preceded by other Blacks bearing bars of gold, would lead the show.

In 1680 a historian wrote: "On the Lion is mounted a young Negro Prince attired in a very right habit... with a fold hilt in scarf of gold by his side. With one hand he holds a golden bridle; in the other St. George's Banner and representeth power."

It is possible to go further back than the middle of the sixteenth century and find historical documents to prove that even as early as 1501 there were Blacks at court in Scotland. That year one of the King's minstrels was "Peter the Moryen or Moor."

One of the first recorded instances of Blacks living south of the border was the return, in 1554, of the London trader John Lok from a voyage to the West Coast of Africa, bringing with him a cargo of five African slaves, "whereof some were tall and strong men." They were taught the language in order that they might be used by merchants plying the slave trade. The Blacks seem to have taken quickly to English food and life. But, Lok said, "the colde and moist aire doth somewhat offend them."

From the time that such English merchants began taking part in the African Slave Trade, the presence of Blacks

82

in England began to increase slowly. To add to their number, Black musicians, like those associated with the commedia dell'arte and the courts of Italian princes, performed in Elizabethan entertainments.

Even at this early stage the government began to show concern over the number of Blacks in England. On August 11, 1596, the Acts of Privy Council stated:

> Her Majestie understanding that there are of late divers Blackamoors brought to this realm, of which kinde of people there are already too manie, considering how God hath blessed this land with great increase of people of our own nation...
> those kinde of people should be sent forth of the land ......

William Shakespeare followed the tradition of the times in his melodramatic tragedy *Titus Andronicus*, first performed sometime between 1590 and 1592. This play goes to extremes and exploits the contemporary taste for gruesome spectacle and violence, making of Black evil and creating the stereotype. Rape, mutilation and death are depicted in lavish amounts, usually through the machinations of the Black villain, Aaron. His bodily Blackness is etched plainly for all to see; and he is described at sundry times as "raven-coloured," "a Black devil," and a "coal Black Moor." He himself refers to "my fleece of wooly hair." He performs his evil doings as a form of revenge with relish and glee: Hear his comment:

> O, how this villainy,
> Doth fat me with the very thought of it.
> Let fools do good and fair men call for grace.

In one memorable scene Aaron appears in a more sympathetic light. The Nurse produces Aaron's baby, "a joyless, dismal and sorrowful issue" and Tamora's order is that the child should be destroyed. Aaron refuses, seizes the child, defies Demetrius and Charon, and stabs the Nurse. He carries off the child, "this treasure in mine arms." In defending his son for that moment he becomes a representative of his race, protesting against prejudice; he asks: Is Black so base a hue? Then he turns to Tamora's wretched sons:

> Ye White-timid walls! Ye alehouse painted signs!
> Coal-Black is better than another hue!

The villain becomes hero at that moment. Aaron is the only character in this play of atrocities that attains a certain vitality, and in this capacity he belongs to the tradition of the villain-hero. In Elizabethan drama no one will dispute the fact that the Black man was always depicted as villain. Consequently, it must have had a startling impact on Shakespeare's audience to see a Black hero of outstanding qualities in the play Othello – one of the great tragedies.

The plot of *Othello* hinges on the fact of Othello's Blackness, especially as he marries a beautiful White Desdomona. It is this situation that exposes the torrent of racist behavior that Othello receives primarily at the hands of Iago, a paranoid, evil, White villain who was thoroughly jealous of the Black Prince. Even in the end, when Desdemona is killed by Othello in a fit of jealousy, the sympathies of the audience for Othello are never completely destroyed. This comes about because, in *Othello*, Shakespeare presents his Elizabethan audience with a series of propositions that serve to reverse or disturb their set notions of Black people. First of all, a Christian African is pitted against what has been described as "a diabolical White, a startling reversal of the norm." An honorable and self-restrained African is also set against a sensual, debased White who lusts after the African's wife; once again a reversal of the situation found in plays like *Lust's Dominion*. Finally, a mature African male of modest sexual inclination and ability is wedded to a youthful White female who openly exposes a bold sexual appetite. It is this last contradiction of the norm that remains at the heart of the play.

In other plays, too, William Shakespeare ignores the conventions of the day in presenting African characters. For instance, in *Love's Labour's Lost*, when the king tells Biron that his love, Rosaline, "is as Black as ebony" and that "Black is the badge of hell," he answers back: "As ebony like her? O wood divine. No fair that is not full so Black... And therefore is she born to make Black hair". The exchange of words between the King and Biron ends in favor of a Black skin over a White one, with the King himself speaking of "the sweet complexion of the Ethiopes."

Another instance – and one could cite several more – which shows clearly Shakespeare's positive interest and approach to African characters, can be found in *Troilus and Cressida*. Pandarus says of the beautiful Cressida, "I care not if she were a Blackamoor."

A further striking example of this attitude occurs in *The Two Gentlemen of Verona*. Thurio, Proteus, and Julia, who is beloved of Proteus, enter into the palace of the Duke of Milan. For their conversation "Black" is made out to be attractive:

Thurio: What says she to my face?
Proteus: She says it is a fair one.
Thurio: Nay then, the wanton lies; My face is Black.
Proteus: But Pearls are fair; and the old saying is
Black men are pearls in beauteous ladies' eyes.
Julia: Tis True.

There is absolutely no doubt that William Shakespeare's love of dark-skinned characters was of a personal and emotional nature. In a London crowded with Africans, Shakespeare came into close contact with them, a contact that resulted with his love affair with one of them, Lucy Negro. Out of that affair came the writing of the *Dark Lady of The Sonnets.*

There has been an ongoing controversy in scholarly circles as to the identity of the Dark Lady in Shakespeare's Sonnets. Claims have been made for some White women purely because they were brunettes and had dark eyes. Among the three most spoken of are high-spirited Mary Fitton, a maid of honor to Queen Elizabeth I; the then-innkeeper's wife, Mrs. Davenant; and finally, Anne Whateley of Temple Grafton, a village six miles away from Stratford-upon-Avon. Most prominent among the scholars who laid these claims was Ivor Brown, who did not deny that these ladies' claims rested on their brunette hair and dark eyes, and that they moved in circles in which Shakespeare was said to have been. If we examine the words of Shakespeare, in his Sonnets to the Dark Lady, we can arrive at but one conclusion, as did scholars, like Dr. George Bagshawe Harrison, Dr. Leslie Hotson, poet Terence Tiller and others.

In his Sonnets to the Dark Lady, Shakespeare begins by defending her color. In Sonnet 127 he writes:

> In the old age Black was not counted fair, or if it
> were, it bore not beauty's name; but now is Black
> beauty's successive heir.

So that there shall be no doubts as to the racial origin of his Dark Lady, he gives this description of her in Sonnet 130:

> If hairs be wires, Black wires grow on her head. I
> have seen roses damask'd red and White, but no
> such roses see I in her cheeks.

No one in his or her right senses would describe Englishwoman's hair as wiry; you know where texture of hair would be most likely found. If the Dark Lady had been English, her cheeks probably have had the peaches-and-cream complexion usually associated with the Englishwoman. Shakespeare could find no such bloom on his mistress's cheeks. Evidence exists that Lucy Negro or, to call her by her other name, Luce Morgan, did charm William Shakespeare. So, we can come to no other conclusion but to agree with other scholars, and in the words of Dr. George Bagshawe Harrison, in his book *Shakespeare At Work*:

> In the Gray's Inn revels, amongst those brought in to pay homage to the Prince of Purpool was Lucy Negro of Clerkenwell. This Lucy Negro I would identify as the Dark Lady.

REFERENCES:

Dabydeen, David, ed., *The Black Presence in English Literature* (Manchester University Press, 1985)

Faggett, Harry Lee, *Black and other Minorities in Shakespeare's England* (Texas: Prairie View, 1971)

Harrison, G.B., *Shakespeare at Work: 1592-1603* (London, 1933)

Hotson, Leslie, *Mr. W.H.* (London, 1964)

Jones, Eldred, *Othello's Countrymen* (London: OUP, 1965)

Scobie, Edward, "Shakespeare's Dark Lady of the Sonnets," *BBC Broadcast,* 7 May 1957
———— "The African Pearl," *BBC Broadcast,* 6 March 1959
———— *Black Britannia* (Chicago: Johnson Publishing, 1972)

Van Sertima, Ivan, ed., *African Presence in Early Europe* (New Brunswick, NJ: Transaction Books, 1985)

CHAPTER FIVE

African Women In Early Europe

For this work, and any other study of such nature, Britain must be included since, culturally and historically, that country belongs to the European continent. It has been through cultural changes that bear certain similarities to those geographically located on the European landmass. As far as African women are concerned, then, the history of Britain, like that of the other European countries, is replete with the full measure of their presence and attitudes to them. These, not surprisingly, have almost never found their way into the pages of European scholarship. The odd times when they have are always tinted by pens mired in racism.

In the age of the Crusades, Europe began to develop consciousness as a geopolitical entity and at the same time to become dimly conversant of Africans as a separate race in the human community. Early contacts (1000-1450) through Spain were made with Africans as "humble slaves and wild warriors." In the Middle Ages, although the world of Islam was wedged in between Christendom and the land of Africa, contact between the two continents was made at three spots: in Spain from Morocco Sudan; from land in Italy through Sicily, Tunis and Cyrenaica; and through Jerusalem from the lands of the Nile (Egypt, Ethiopia and Sudan). It is from these contacts that emerged the European's medieval image of the African. In Spain there were African soldiers and servants among the Moslem conquerors ever since Tarik invaded the Iberian peninsula in 711 A.D.

Professor Verlinden of Ghent University has made what he describes as a careful study about African slaves in both Moslem and Christian Iberia. He states that in the eleventh and twelfth centuries, there was a substantial increase in African slaves in Moslem Spain as well as in North Africa. The increase in African slaves in the eleventh and twelfth centuries can be attributed to the Almoravid conquest of Spain. History has shown that the politico-religious movement of the Almoravids had its origins on the western fringes of the Sahara and it fanned out with their conquest of the famous African kingdom of Ghana in the Sudan by 1086. It was the plundered gold of ancient Ghana and the bravery of the Sudanese soldiers that helped to conquer Spain. A sizable number of Africans fought in the Moslem armies of the peninsula and they literally frightened the Christians with their acts of daring. That is why the African presence in Moslem Spain made a profound mark on the art and literature of the times. The exoticism of the African as someone different was the European view in this first attempt to integrate the African into European cultural awareness. At this time miscegenation took place on an ever widening scale, hence accounting for a very large percentage of African blood in the Spanish people. The Spaniards took the African strain further into Europe, in France and the former Netherlands. When they were driven out of these lands, roughly 3000 of them settled in Hamburg, and many a Hamburg citizen bears a striking resemblance to the Spanish, with black wavy, curly hair and swarthy skin.

Evidence of Blacks in Germany has been claimed to date back to the Neanderthal skull, the oldest African type in Europe discovered in Dusseldorf in 1856, and said to belong to the Old Stone Age. The Grimaldis, an African people, lived in Europe over 12,000 years ago. Evidence of their presence and culture has been unearthed in Southern and Central Europe. Two complete skeletons of the Grotte des Enfants are in a complete state of preservation in the Museum of Monaco, near

Monte Carlo.

Julius Caesar brought Black legions into Germany and Britain. The skull of an ancient African was found at Cologne, a Christian martyr whose head had been pierced by a nail. The Huns, a dark Mongolian people, overran Europe in the fourth and fifth centuries and contributed much to the present stock of German people. This makes a mockery of the purebred Aryan German race about whom Adolf Hitler fantasized in his racist distorted work *Mein Kampf.*

Portugal itself has been described by historians, particularly Brunold Springer, as "the first example of Negrito (African) Republic in Europe." He went on to write in his book Racial Mixture as the Basic Principle of Life:

> In the Portuguese runs a deep current of Negro blood, and there the Negro has often risen to the caste of the nobility. Napoleon's army had many Black Portuguese soldiers ... Sicily, of course, is also profoundly Africanised. All of this is ancient history. The Romans brought Negro troops to the Rhine and over the Donau. Later merchants purchased the young Negroes as servants; in all large cities of commerce there were several hundred Blacks, and many a house was known simply as "at the Moors." In one circle of people whose members belong to the Russian, English and German nobility there is much Negro blood inherited from an ancestor who lived at the end of the eighteenth century, and who was the great grandfather of one of the greatest poets of all lands and of all times, Alexander Sergeivitch Pushkin.

One of the well-known examples of a member of royalty with the blood of Africa coursing in her veins was Queen Charlotte Sophia, German-born consort of the

English King George 111 (1760-1820). She had the broad nostrils and heavy lips of the blond Negroid type mentioned by Brunold Springer. This type is not uncommon even in Nordic Europe where intermixing, as mentioned previously, has been taking place from the earliest antiquity. These facts of history have never been given partial or full exposure in the writings of Europeans for obvious racist reasons.

Another royal queen with the blood of Africa in her veins is the Duchess of Alafoes. She was described as the most beautiful woman at the court of John VI of Portugal in the 1800s, by a noble French authoress. Voicing paeans of praise about the beauty of the Duchess, she exclaimed: "The Duchess is brown but comely." The Duchess was the King's aunt. At that time fully one-third of Portugal was Black (African). Hence this question of pure race among Europeans was nothing but a myth in order to perpetuate the fantasy of a "superior" race. H.G. Wells, the English writer and historian, wrote:

> "Everyone alive is, I am convinced, of mixed ancestry, but some of us are more White, some of us more Negro, some of us more Chinese."

The sex relations between White and Black go back to very early times and on all continents. In that respect Europe was well ahead of the others in those distant times.

There can be no denying that the African woman in Europe was viewed in different lights, either as a Goddess or a courtesan, or a wife, or a mistress. At the other, more spiritual level, she was likened to a Madonna, the mother of Jesus; this, too, being part of the mold just described. Hence the cult of the Black Madonna and Child that has dominated the Catholic world, particularly of Europe, has been recognized and venerated by Catholics up to this day. One of the most devoted pilgrims at the shrine of the Black Madonna was the late Pope

John Paul II. Two of the oldest Black Madonnas of Europe are those of Loretto, Italy and of Nuria, Spain. The first has been listed as the original of all the Black Madonnas. It was destroyed by fire around 1930 and restored by Pope Pius XI who, according to Father Hedit, insisted that the color be preserved. The Black Madonna of Nuria is known as "The Queen of the Pyrenees."

One of the very earliest manifestations of the Black Goddess syndrome was the Venus of Willendorf (15000-10000 B.C.), found near Vienna, Austria. It was carved by Blacks of the Grimaldi peoples living in Europe, and is the oldest known representation of the human body. It is now in the Vienna Museum. We find this theme of the Black Goddess, the Black Venus carried from century to century in Europe right down to the years of the slave trade and slavery. The Oracle of Dodona in Greece, the place where the gods were consulted, was founded by two Black women.

Herodotus stated:

> two Black doves had come flying from Thebes .. one to Libya and one to Dodona she taught divination, as soon as she understood the Greek language ... these women were called "doves" by the people of Dodona because they spoke a strange language, and the people thought it like the cries of birds (only certain African languages have this sound) ... The tale that the dove was Black signifies that the women were Egyptian.

As the story of the African woman in Europe travels through the centuries, several cases of the conflicting attitudes of Europeans will come to the fore. The same thing applies to the British in their relationship with Blacks.

London in the time of Shakespeare was teeming with Africans, and there were large numbers of African women living there, particularly in the Clerkenwell area of the city. They were much courted by the young, better-class men around town: lawyers, actors, musicians, writers, and the nobility. In a letter dated 1602, one Dennis Edwards writes to Thomas Lankford, secretary to the Earl of Hertford, asking: "Pray enquire and secure my negress;" and went on to give the address where his lady love was to be found.

Situations of this nature, in which African women were being seen, existed elsewhere in Europe from the fifteenth and sixteenth centuries onward, in Germany, Italy, and France, Spain, and Portugal. The case of Isabeau, an African, born in the Motherland, carried in slave chain to the Caribbean, and taken out of the plantations of Haiti to Paris, was a classic one. She caused a tremendous sensation in France during the reign of Louis XV (known as the Boy King in the early years of the eighteenth century). With her taste in dress and the wealth she acquired as a result of her exotic charm and superb physical beauty, she became the most sought after woman in France. French aristocrats fell at the feet of this Black goddess. Among those under her spell was the Comte d'Artois, later to become the King of France. Madame du Barry, herself a beauty and favorite of King Louis XV though jealous of Isabeau, was forced to grudgingly admit that:

> Isabeau was proclaimed a charming creature and more than one grand personage of the Court, more than one financier placed his heart and his purse at her feet. Rare and magnificent adornments; great luxury; jewels and precious stones; a natural taste in dress; an accent, piquant because of its strangeness; numerous servants; great sums of money to spend, helped to decide the success of Isabeau. Whenever she came to Versailles to see the King at dinner, there was a great crowd to see her.

The high point of her love life was her rendezvous with the Prince, the Comte d'Artois, at his retreat at Bagatelle. Du Barry and Isabeau became fast friends, the two most beautiful women in France; one White and the other Black. In her memoirs, Madame Du Barry devoted a whole chapter to the African beauty. Even though some of the writing is clouded by a snide remark about color, the impression conveyed is that Isabeau was a beautiful African woman:

> That African woman was charming. Imagine her: tall, supple but voluptuous, with a walk that was elegance itself. Her well-shaped eyes were alive; her mouth admirably formed; her skin was something between satin and velvet; and the most beautiful ears that one could see. Indeed, I must admit that she merited her reputation.

Isabeau was by no means the only favorite in royal circles in France. It was vogue in Europe during those times for high and wealthy personages to have African mistresses. Francis I of France had one; so did Louis XV. She was Mademoiselle St. Hilaire from the Caribbean. There was a son from this union who claimed the throne of France. Louis XVI always chose an African beauty to be his current amour. Historian J. Michelet stated that the first lover of Louis XIV, (1643-1715), the Sun King, was an African woman named Jeanne. His wife, Queen Maria-Theresa of Spain, was to pay him back in his own coins when she took an African lover, Nabo, with serious consequences.

This license was extended to African men, as well, whose sexual favors were sought even in the bedchambers of queens. The case of Marie-Therese, Louis XIV's queen, caused the most concern. It became one of the best-known scandals to travel down from the sixteenth through the nineteenth centuries' lanes of history, and to find exposure even in the remaining few years of the twentieth century. Naturally, excuses were bandied about to save the honor of the Queen, but none stuck. The real story was whispered in the corridors of Versailles, and spoken out loudly and openly in the salons and streets of Paris, the town and village lanes, and the byways and highways of the French countryside. The accepted version of what actually happened between Queen Maria-Theresa and her attendant, Nabo, reads as follows:

> Nabo who come from Dahomey was given to the Queen Maria-Theresa as a gift by M. de Beaufort, as was the custom in those days. The Black teenage young man was dwarfish in height but very well proportioned. The Queen had him to attend her in her bedchamber, growing very fond of him. She kissed, cuddled and fondled him. A lonely woman left to her own devices by the philandering of her royal consort, the plain rather plump Marie-Therese sought solace and comfort in the very amusing and considerate Nabo. He danced attendance on every whim and caprice of his royal mistress. An intimate and strange relationship grew out of the loneliness of the lives of these two unwanted souls; a relationship, which brought about a scandal that was to rock the whole of France, and indeed the rest of Europe.

Marie-Therese was about to become a mother again but this time she became more and more restless and worried. She kept repeating: "I no longer recognize myself. I experience strange disgusts and caprices such as never happened before. If I were to do as I wanted to, I would be cutting somersaults on the carpet, like my little Negro."

The King replied: "Ah, Madame, you make me shiver. Forget your foolish fancies or you will have a child, bizarre and unnatural."

The King was right. When the baby was born in 1656 it was of a dark brown African color. The King become almost hysterical with rage and began stamping and storming about the rooms of the palace. The Queen, as was to be expected, kept swearing her innocence. Doctors tried their level best to pacify the King and assured him that the baby was atavistic, a throwback. The King was on the point of accepting this biologically impossible story when someone mentioned the Queen's attendant, Nabo. "Why," exclaimed one of the doctor, "the color of the child might have been caused by the Black man's looking at the Queen." "A look!" shouted the King. "It must have been a very penetrating look." Then, he ordered Nabo to be brought in his presence. Someone declared, "He is dead, your Majesty." Actually, Nabo had been spirited away some little while before this occasion of the birth. The story was told that he died suddenly, and very soon after the Queen gave birth to his daughter; a daughter who was named Louise-Marie, a compound of the names of both the King and Queen. The sudden death of Nabo, an otherwise healthy young African in the prime of a life that had decades of years ahead of it, remained an unexplained mystery, like the life of his daughter Louise-Marie. It is not too fanciful to surmise that Nabo's death was not of natural, but almost certainly of unnatural causes.

Mademoiselle de Montpensir, the King's cousin and someone intimate in court circles, gave a firsthand account of what actually did take place at the birth of the child:

The Dauphin told me of the trouble they had with the illness of the Queen and the crowds that were there when the King arrived; how the Bishop of Gardes, his first almoner, now Bishop of Langres, almost fainted with sorrow because the Prince and everybody laughed; that the Queen had been angry, and that the royal infant that had just been born, resembled a little Negro dwarf that M. de Beaufort had brought her from foreign lands- little Negro that the Queen always had with her ...; that the child would not live and that I should not mention it to the Queen. When the Queen was a little better I went every day to the Louvre to see her. She told me that everyone had laughed at seeing the child, and the great pain their laughter had caused her.

The child lived and as mentioned elsewhere was named Louise-Marie. So as not to cause further embarrassment the King and Queen and to the country, Louise-Marie was whisked in secret far away, to the convent of Moret, and placed in the care of the Mother Superior and her nuns. The King ordered absolute secrecy. The child was kept a virtual prisoner and not allowed go out. She grew up in the convent and became a nun. However, she still pined for her freedom and restoration to what she believed was her rank. The story goes that one day, when the Dauphin heir to the throne of France was hunting in a nearby forest, and Louise-Marie learnt who the heir was, she burst into tears and said: "It is my brother."

Of this period in the life of Louise-Marie–who became known as The Black Nun–the Duke of St. Simon, a statesman and one of the top figures in the King's Court, wrote:

> Speaking of the secrets of the King, it is necessary to make amends for something else I had forgotten. Everyone was astonished at Fontainebleau this year, to see that hardly had the princess arrived than Mme. de Maintenon took her to the little convent of Moret, where there were likely to be no amusements or persons of her acquaintance. She returned there several times, which awoke curiosity and rumors–Mme. Maintenon went often to Fontainebleau and finally one got accustomed to seeing her go there.
>
> In the convent was a professed nun, a Negro woman, unknown to everyone and who never

showed herself to anyone. Bontemps, first valet to the King and governor of Versailles, to whom I have spoken and to whom the domestic secrets are known, had placed her there quite young after paying a large sum, and a regular pension. He took great care that everything that could add to her comfort was provided. The Queen went often to Fontainebleau to see her, and after her, Mme de Maintenon. The Dauphin went there several times and the princess and the children, and all asked for this Negro woman and treated her with kindness. She was receiving more marks of distinction than the best known or most distinguished person there.

Legends began to grow around the Black Nun. She was honored "as one of those Black Madonnas attributed to St. Luke, who performed miracles and attracted pilgrims." Yet there was another, more colorful aspect to her fascinating mysterious life. She was involved in one of the most romantic love stories of later years. It was claimed that the King's nephew, the Duke of Chartres, fell violently in love with her during a visit to the convent and spirited her away. When the King refused to give his consent to a marriage, the Duke was compelled to take her back to the convent at Moret, where she remained until her death in 1732.

Many were the stories and legends that grew around The Black Nun, Louise-Marie, daughter of Queen Maria-Theresa, who was the wife of the Sun King Louis XIV, and the queen's African lover, Nabo. Louise-Marie's portrait was hung in the art gallery of the Library of St. Genevieve in the Latin Quarter of Paris. It shows her to be a beautiful Black woman (prettier than her mother, the queen) with bright black eyes, a prominent nose, thick lips and a long chin. The lower part of her face is unmistakably Africoid. Specimens of her handwriting have been preserved, although the original documents detailing her birth and background disappeared as silently and mysteriously

PRINCESS MARIE-LOUISE
Daughter of Louise XIV and Queen Maria-Theresa

as her African father, Nabo. All that was rescued from isolation, and is at the Library of Genevieve, was the cover in which the documents were kept. It bears the title: "Documents concerning The Princess Louise-Marie, daughter of Louis XIV and Marie-Therese." Thus history records that Louis XIV, a White King of France, through sexual union with his White Queen, Marie-Therese, fathered an African daughter!

Going further back into the years of antiquity from as far back as 1000 A.D., and even further, right up to 1450, the century before Shakespeare, we discern the presence of African playing a most striking role on the scene. And when we talk about Europe in that slot of time we must be precise as to which areas we are referring. Also, we must define and categorize the racial intermixing that took place in Europe from earliest times. Many people do not realize how recently the concept of "Europe" came into being. Historians R.R. Palmer and Joel Colton wrote, in their book *A History of the Modern World:*

> There was really no Europe in ancient times. In the Roman Empire we may see a Mediterranean world or even a West and East in the Latin-and Greek-speaking portions. But the West included parts of Africa as well as of Europe, and Europe as we know it was divided by the Rhine-Danube frontier, south and west of which lay the civilized provinces of the Empire, and north and east the "barbarians" of whom the civilized world knew almost nothing.

In fact Palmer and Colton maintain in their study that the word "Europe" was scarcely ever used by the Romans at all, since it meant little to them. In very earliest times, when we say Europe, we are really referring to the Graeco-Roman areas of civilization since tribes to the north and east had produced nothing in the field of enlightenment other than the area was the habitat of "barbarians." In the interest of truth it is imperative to remove the European mystique around the Graeco-Roman Empire in those ancient times. Europe gets the credit for culture, civilization and enlightenment of this empire when, in historical fact, that was not the case. Europe, as the world was wrongly led to perceive it, just was not in existence as the home base of culture and civilization. In the words of the Ugandian scholar Professor Ali A. Mazuri, of Makerere University:

> It is at any rate time that it was more openly conceded not only that ancient Egypt made a contribution to the Greek miracle, but also that she in turn had been influenced by the Africa which was to the south of her. To grant all this is, in a sense, to universalize the Greek heritage. It is to break the European monopoly of identification with ancient Greece.

The logic of this statement by Professor Mazuri remains quite obvious: that ancient Greece was not, in a real sense, European since it owed most of its cultural heritage to the Africanness of Egypt, Ethiopia and Sudan. Take, for instance, Sappho, the sixth century B.C. poet who has been accepted as the best lyric poet of Greece. The Greeks admired her poetry to such an extent that she was called "The Tenth Muse." She described herself as Black, an African.

Greek gods and goddesses, and much of what is known as Greek Mythology, have been borrowed or, to be more explicit, extracted from Egypt and other Nile Valley countries. In fact, much more than that which has been credited to the Greeks – philosophy, mathematics, science, medicine, law, etc. – had roots dug out of the Nile Valley civilization and culture, and made to look as if they came from the Greeks. Most of the gods and goddesses of Greece were of Egyptian origin, which is African origin. The Muses have been described as the daughters of Ethiopia. To reinforce this claim, the Greek historian Herodotus has stated that, "Almost all of the names of gods came into Greece from Egypt."

Zeus, known as the father of all the gods, was of African ancestry. He sired a son named Epaphus. The great Aeschylus, tragic Greek poet, said of Zeus, "And thou shalt bring forth Black Epaphus," thus named from the manner of Zeus engendering. One of the titles of Zeus was Ethiop, signifying Black (Africa).

Among the Greek goddesses, Diana of Attica was Black and an Ethiopian. It was Apollo who took her away from her country. Not only did the Greeks claim African gods and goddesses, but they also worshipped them and paid homage to them, as beings of a higher level, higher than the ordinary morality of men and women: beings who were capable of acts above the capability of man born out of a woman. In other words, their hero and heroine images and role models from antiquity to today have been based upon the images of Africans. African women, as a result, were more favored among Greeks than their own. They were viewed in a variety of ways, with the sex motif almost always a factor. It ruled the passions and attitudes of Greek men in the arts, literature and in their social behavior.

It was in the Greek city of Corinth where a Black Venus was adored and glorified for her beauty and charm as the symbol of love. One of the best-known Venus figures in Europe is that of the Black Venus by the Italian artist Alessandro Vittoria (1525-1608). Incidentally, the goddess image of Venus, or Aphrodite as she is also known, was taken from the Egyptian goddess Hathor. When Europeans say a Black Venus, they are making a statement that is chronologically incorrect. In fact, in their mythology, the most famous female magician of all time, Circe, played a great role in Homer's *Odyssey*. Ancient Greek drawings depict her as a beautiful African woman. To her

ARTEMIS, GODDESS OF CHASTITY

was attributed the power of turning human beings into lower animals. It was she who changed the companions of Ulysses, the Greek hero-warrior, into hogs.

It was evident that African women were the favorites of Greek poets. One poet praised them to the skies, saying: "With her charms Didymee has ravished my heart. Alas I melt as wax at the sight of her beauty. She is Black, it is true, but what matters? Coals are Black; but when they are alight they glow like rose cups." Such praise was commonplace among Greek poets.

Greek lovers of the African woman did not restrict their worship only to the love-sex vision. There were contradictions. The Greeks saw other virtues in African women, virtues not directly related to the passions of the flesh that the Black female body incited in them. For instance, their Goddess of Chastity, Artemis, was Black. The Greeks chose an African princess, Minerva, to represent their Goddess of Wisdom; thus placing the African woman not only as an object of sex, but as a virtuous, spiritual and intellectual being capable of elevating man to loftier heights.

Following in that tradition through the centuries, we find some African women who were deeply religious and endowed with mystical powers. For instance, in Spain in the 1700s an African girl from Guinea named Chicava became one of the leading religious figures. Adopted by the Emperor Charles II at the age of nine, she was christened Teresa Juliana. She was put in the care of the Marquis Marrera and his wife who brought the girl up as their daughter. When her uncle, the King of Niña Baja, tried to force her hand in marriage, she entered the Convent of La Penitencia, Salamanca. As a nun she became famous for spiritual work, showing that she had miraculous powers. Teresa Juliana died in 1748. Her memory and her relics are still esteemed with veneration. In 1757 an epic poem was written about her life and works. Today she is remembered in Spain and other Catholic countries as La Santa Negrita–The Black Saint.

While there were African women who were mistresses of the highborn in Europe, there were those who were darlings of royalty in other, less carnal relationships. For instance, in 1504 two "Blackamoor" girls were taken to Scotland to the Royal Court, where they were baptized and educated. They were named Ellen and Margaret and waited on the Queen, Margaret of Scotland, as her personal and favorite attendants. Their popularity rose to such heights that in June 1507, a tournament was held in honor of the Queen's Black lady, Ellen Moore, which was conducted with greatest splendor. The highborn White ladies at court could scarcely contain their jealousy.

In the 1850s one of Queen Isabella of Spain's most cherished favorites was an African beauty and guitarist named Maria Marline.

A celebrated case of a royal darling was that of Ismeria, an African woman from the Sudan who married Robert d'Eppes, son of William II of France. There was a son by that marriage named Jean, who became a companion of St. Louis, King of France, during the period of the Crusades. In a chart of 1236, Jean is described as the "son of the Negro woman." Ismeria herself was a notable person who achieved lasting recognition. At her death she was made a Black Madonna. While in the Sudan, she saved many Christian knights from death. Her fame had reached such esteemed proportions that a town sprang up near her shrine, and pilgrims from all parts of France came to pay homage to her with rich presents. Among those who came to worship at her shrine were Joan of Arc, Louis XI and Francis I. She is remembered as Notre Dame de Liesse.

Black women were the most talked about, sought after and courted women in Europe from the time Europe made contact with Africa. European men of all ranks could not resist their charm, which was mysterious, spiritual, and contained just enough sensuality to uncover the passions of European men and have them paying homage. Not only were these African women objects of passion, but wives, goddesses and madonnas, as well.

In 1413 Anselme d'Ysaguirre, a French nobleman and member of Parliament in Toulouse, France, fell deeply in love with the beautiful 20-year-old daughter of a king, Salem-Casais from Gao, Songhay. Salem-Casais gave birth to a lovely daughter named Martha. When the child grew up she became belle of Toulouse. Their descendants married into some of the leading families in Toulouse; families that have grown through the centuries and are in existence up until this present time. Traces of Africa have disappeared in this and literally hundreds of thousands of such families in Europe and also in Britain. This is a historical fact that should be made known to those Whites who are forever shouting about a pure White race. In the words of more sensible White scholars, such a condition does not exist, never did, and never will.

One of the most celebrated cases of an African woman who won the attention of a venerated member of Italian society was Anna. She was to enter into the service of Alfonsina Orsini, a near relative of the Cardinal dei Medici, who became Pope Clement VII. Out of this association with the Medicis a son was born in 1511 named Alessandro dei Medici, the first Duke of Florence, referred to as "the Moor." All the writers of the period agree that Alessandro was of African origin and his portrait by Bronzino reflects this fact. In 1536 Alessandro married Margaret, daughter of Charles V, emperor of Germany, Spain and Austria. Alessandro's mother, Anna, was so beautiful that she was called the Italian Cleopatra.

"NEGRESS MOUNTING A HORSE"
Robert Auguste Portrait

The vogue for African women was most manifest in the works of writers, poets and artists. It was always fashionable for artists to paint or sculpt the African woman in all her beauty and glory. In fact, the presence of the African woman in Europe was to impact visibly on all sectors of the society.

From the Renaissance painters to the seventeenth, eighteenth and nineteenth century artists, the African woman in Europe was a favorite. African children and men were also very popular and were frequently painted by some of the most celebrated painters: Rubens, Hogarth, Zoffany, Gainborough, Reynolds, Watteau, and many others too numerous to list.

Qualities most evident in many of the paintings of African women by Europeans are sensuality and sex. For instance, William Hogarth (1697-1764) the prolific British artist, shows in his painting entitled "An Unpleasant Discovery" the friends of an English dandy discovering that he has a Black woman in his luxurious bed. Incidentally, this painting is omitted from most editions of Hogarth's work. However, a copy appears in Iwan Bloch's *Sex Life in England*. In one of his other paintings titled "The Rake's Progress," Hogarth paints an African girl witnessing a scene of profligacy. Sir Joshua Renolds (1723-1792), in one of his famous portraits in private possession at Woburn Abbey, has a full-bosomed African woman contrasting her natural beauty with the "noble" beauty of the marchioness, Lady Elizabeth Keppel. In one of his best portraits, titled "Negress Mounting a Horse," the French eighteenth century artist Robert Auguste shows a physical study of a nude African woman about to mount a stallion. The symbolic meaning and interpretation of his study are quite clear.

On of the most shocking pictures about the African woman to come out of seventeenth-century Europe was painted in 1632 by Christian Van Couwenbergh. Entitled "The Rape of the Negro woman," it shows three White men in a bedchamber who have overpowered and stripped an African woman and are about to rape her. She is struggling to get free. Swiss historian Hans Werner Debrunner described this picture as "revoltingly honest." He went on to say, "In a dramatic way, the painter accuses Europeans of brutal abuse of Africans." Debrunner, after looking at the paintings of African women by European artists, gives his interpretation and summary of attitudes. He states that:

> The African woman belongs to the dream-world of primal psychological conceptions ... All these representations and descriptions of African women show a common tendency: to imagine in African woman a being sometimes dangerous, sometimes amusing, always different and possibly even doomed to perdition.

While this may well have been the sum total of the European artists' conception of the African woman in Debrunner's view, it still omits another aspect of the African woman brought out by many European artists: the spiritual, madonna-like qualities, and the Black Venus and Black Goddess image which have remained. This other conception of those European artists cannot be used as a yardstick to judge with any accuracy the realities of the situation of the African woman in European society. She was mistress, mother, lover, and wife to the highest in that continent. More than that, she was vested with spiritual qualities: chaste, holy, pure, miraculous. In European society she was certainly not "doomed to perdition." She was a woman of inspiration, vested with physical attributes and charm, which shook the thrones of Europe and caused not ripples, but waves, among the most powerful, the most religious, the most artistic.

The case of the young Senegalese girl, Ourika de Beauvau, is one of inspiration. This young African girl was born in the early 1780s and taken to France in 1788. She died

110

in her sixteenth year of what was described as "a mysterious disease." She had been presented to Marshal de Becauvou by the governor of the colony of Senegal, Chevalier Stanislas de Boufflers. She immediately won the affection of this aristocratic family and was adopted as a daughter. When she died, Mme. de Beauvau wrote of her adopted African daughter: "Ourika was much loved. She had charm, beauty, a sweet temper, taste, reticence, spirit." Ourika made such an indelible impression in literary circles of the nobility, that she became the heroine of the novel "Ourika," a work full of imagination and poetic invention.

It is in the poetry of Europe, of Britain, of the world that the African woman has most frequently and liberally been portrayed. In fact, it would not be inaccurate one bit to state that no White, Asian, or other race, has been eulogized in the poetry of the world of Europe, America and elsewhere as the African woman. Poets have left her lasting immortal image: Black Madonna, Black Mother, Black Goddess, Black Venus. When we cast our minds back into the antiquity of Europe these are the images that appear before us. The rest pales in significance. Even during the years of the African Slave Trade, when extremes of humiliation were heaped upon captured Africans, taken to the plantation prisons of the Caribbean and North America, Europeans were penning panegyrics about the Black Venus. Artists, too, used the image of a Black Venus to symbolize the journey from Africa across the Middle Passage to the slave plantations of the Americas and the Caribbean. In 1818 T. Stothard painted a symbolic canvas entitled, "The Voyage of the Sable Venus from Angola, West Africa to the West Indies, Escorted by a White Neptune and a Nimbus White Cupids." This portrait gave poetic expression to the fact that "fanciers of fair Black femininity from Boston, Mass., to Buenos Aires used to await the slave ships for the arrival of these Black Venuses" – to use the words of the immortal J.A. Rogers.

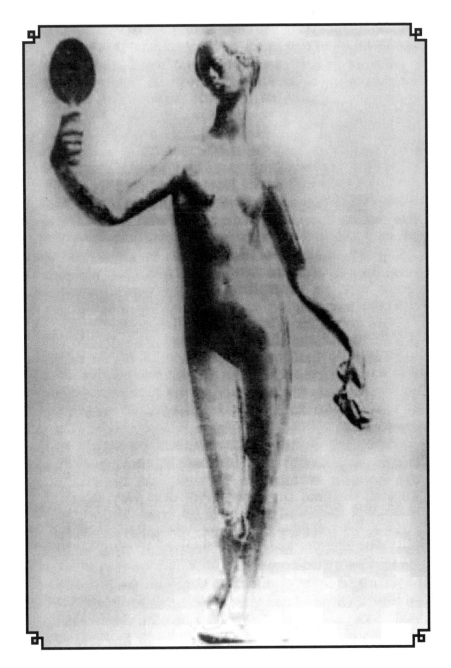

AFRICAN VENUS
By Alessandro Vittoria (1525-1608)

A member of the British Parliament, after seeing Stothard's great painting, "The Black Venus", wrote these ecstatic lines:

Her skin excelled the raven's plume
Her breath the fragrant orange bloom
Her eyes the tropic beam.
Soft was her lip of silken down
And mild her look as evening sun
That gild the cobre stream.

And so the image of the African woman remains enshrined in Europe for all time, for eternity. She cannot be erased from their history or indeed from the history of the world, no matter how hard the Europeans may try to remove her presence. She is there forever, not only as the Black Madonna to be worshipped by Pope John Paul II and millions of other Catholics; but also as the Black Venus, desirable, unattainable; as the beautiful fruit of creation, holding magnetic attraction unattainable to the European man who has always sought to defile her body.

But most important of all, she unmasks the pretense of strength and power in the European man and shows that beneath that veneer of sophistication and might he holds no control over the weakness of his flesh; so that he, too, will always pay homage to her – the African Goddess of the Earth.

REFERENCES:

Hyman, Mark. *Blacks Before America II* (Penn, 1978)

Jackson, John, G. *Introduction To African Civilization* (University Books, 1970)

James, George G.M. *Stolen Legacy* (New York, 1954) *Global Perspective Of Blacks, National Scene New York,* April - May 1975

Ottley, Roi. *No Green Pastures.* London 1952

Reader's Digest, *History Of Man,* New York 1973

Rogers, J.A. *The Real Facts About Ethiopia,* N.Y. 1936

_____. *World's Great Men Of Color,* *Volumes 1 & 2* (New York, 1946-47)

_____. *Nature Knows No Color Line* (New York 1952)

_____. *100 Amazing Facts About The Negro* (New York 1940)

_____. *Sex And Race, Volumes I and II* (New York, 1940)

_____. *Your History* (Black Classic Press, 1983)

Scobie, Edward. *Black Britannia* (Chicago: Johnson Publishing Company, 1972)

Highlights In Black Achievement, Sepia Magazine (Boston: December 1979)

Snowden, Frank M. *Blacks In Antiquity* (Harvard University Press, 1970)

Debrunner, Hans W. *Presence And Prestige: Africans In Europe* (Basel, Switzerland, 1979)

CHAPTER SIX

The Chevalier De Saint-Georges

Titled persons in France and England in the third period of the eighteenth century fawned on him. They called him "the most seductive of coloured gentlemen." Society hostesses sought his company and invited him to their homes and their exclusive parties.

His handsome presence – for he was over six feet and well-built – his talents, his learning, his refinements were of the quality found in gentlemen of breeding. He fascinated everyone who came into contact with him; his color being, more often than not, an attraction rather than a cause for condemnation. There is substantial evidence in the pages of European history (ironically enough) of Africans in that area of the globe, before, during, and after that time, who gained positions of respect and a kind of glory on their merits. The Chevalier de Saint-Georges was one of those favored individuals. British historian Dr. Kenneth Little saw fit to write:

> Colored men who acquired wealth and patronage were received without reservation in the very highest circles. A French mulatto, the Chevalier Georges de Saint-Georges, son of the Marquis de Langley and a Negro slave, was a personal friend of the Prince of Wales, afterwards George IV, and the champion swordsman of his day, and an accomplished rider, skater and violinist, who once set the fashion in the English courts. Until at least well on in the eighteenth century Englishmen saw nothing extraordinary in a Negro possessing talents equal to their own.

What Little stopped at saying was that many Africans possessed talents far superior to those of others who were fair of flesh and blue of eye. In fact, one of the most important talents of the fascinating Chevalier, and one which Little, like some others, by-passed was that the African was one of the major composers in Europe, at a time when there were many European composers upon whom history has bestowed the flame of brilliance and greatness: men like Jean-Marie Leclair, who was reported to have been one of Saint-Georges' tutors; Johann Sebastian Bach; Luigi Boccherni; Franz Joseph Haydn; Karl Stamitz; Wolfgang Amadeus Mozart; and Johann Christian Bach, Bach's youngest son, to name some. Saint-Georges stands alone and supreme as a violin virtuoso and, more importantly, as a composer.

To have been exceptionally gifted as a violinist and as well as a composer who has stood the test immortality, and whose compositions are played constantly on the concert platforms of the classical centers and cities of the world to this day, would have been more than enough in one person. Not so with the Chevalier de Saint-Georges. Just as Imhotep of ancient Kemet (Egypt) was not only the Great Father of Medicine but the foremost architect of his time, the Prime Minister of King Zoser, and worshipped as the Prince of Peace in Rome; the Chevalier was a man of multiple talents. He was the most outstanding man in France and, indeed, in Britain and the rest of Europe in his time. Not one European came anywhere near him. J.A. Rogers, one of the most prolific researchers and historians of Africans, called him the "Dazzling Black Nobleman of Versailles" and went on in words of the noblest praise:

> The adventures of Chevalier de Saint-Georges were so astonishing, his talents so superlatively brilliant, that an account of his life reads like an incredibly romantic novel with a perfect hero. He

was the most dazzling and fascinating figure at the most splendid court in Europe. As a violinist, pianist, poet, musical composer, and actor he was phenomenal; as a swordsman he so far eclipsed the best of his time that in his prime none could match him; as a marksman none could pull a trigger with such unerring aim; as a soldier and commander he performed prodigious feats on the field of battle; as a dancer, swimmer, horseman, and skater he was the most graceful in a land supreme for its grace and elegance; in the matter of dress he was the model of his day, setting the fashions of England and France; a King of France, a future King of England, and Royal Princes sought his company, and to crown all he possessed a spirit of rare generosity, kindness and rectitude.

In today's papers and journals, whenever and wherever his compositions are recorded or played, the chorus of voices sing his praises. In the New York Times of January 24, 1982, Donal Henahan in his article "The Composer as Musketeer," stated:

> It is certain that Saint-Georges was an exceptional violinist as well as an athlete and adventurer in the D' Artagnan style...[He] founded and conducted one of France's great orchestras, and composed stacks of concertos, symphonies and other works. His own concertos they make extensive use of the highest positions and require phenomenal agility in crossing the strings and in multiple stopping, often in the quickest of tempos ... The dashing composer-soldier was a composer virtuoso in the swashbuckling style.

In 1840, a historical novel written by one Roger de Beauvoir highlighted the exciting romantic life of Saint-Georges. This work, though couched in the novel form, was described as "factually reliable" and has been a source of some information to biographers and others in putting the grandiose life of this universal African in print. Several other major sources exist, and these, too, have been examined and utilized copiously in this current work.

Before examining the life of the Chevalier in deeper and more minute detail, it is necessary to hammer home, yet one more time, the greatness of this magnificent African. Joel-Marie Fauquet, a French musicologist in writing about Saint-Georges and his unique concertos had this to write (the translation here is by Charles Whitfield):

> His contemporaries were in agreement as regards his elegance, purity, expression, his talent "moelleux" [mellow] (an adjective used by many of them to describe him.) A chronicler added "His superiority on the violin sometimes gave him preference over, the most accomplished artists of his time."

Who, then, was this larger than life and ten times more talented African who scintillated the courts of pre-Revolutionary eighteenth century Paris? Where did he come from? What was his background?

Joseph Boulogne, Chevalier de Saint-Georges, was born on the French Caribbean island of Guadeloupe, near the village of Bosse Terre. It was during the seventeenth century of French colonization that Joseph-Jean-Nicholas Boulogne (Boulonge or Boullogne) came to the island from France. He had held a position in the Parliament at Metz, and was then appointed Comptroller and Secretary to the Ordre de Saint-Espirit. Monsieur Boulogne owned property near Basse Terre – an estate called Les Polmiers. He had also acquired land known as La Rose in another Caribbean island, Saint Dominique (later to become Haiti). It was this high-placed

French gentleman who was the father of Saint-Georges. His mother was known as the beautiful Nanon and described by those who knew her in glowing terms: "She was considered one of the finest women that Africa had ever sent to the plantations." Saint-Georges was born of a passionate love affair between this Comptroller General of Guadeloupe and the beautifully but lowly African taken to the island in captivity.

The child of this liaison was born in 1739 and not on Christmas day, 1745, as had been originally reported. Saint-Georges, in the words of a biographer, was named after a superbly handsome ship that rode at anchor in the port at Basse Terre during the occasion of his birth. The baby was baptized not too long afterward in the presence of his mother Nanon, by the priest of St. Mark's in Saint Dominique on the island of Hispaniola. As was customary in Catholic countries, baptism took place fairly soon after the boy's birth. What was also evident was that both father and mother had already moved from Guadeloupe into Saint Dominique. It would seem, then, that the sugar plantation La Rose in Saint Dominique was purchased by Boulogne after Saint-Georges was born.

The parents seemed to have remained on that island, Hispaniola – of which one-third (the western part) consisted of the country of Saint Dominique – for some years. For it was there that Saint-Georges began studying the violin at the tender age of five under Joseph Platon (1710- c.1763), who was said to be a poor teacher but the owner of an excellent violin previously the property of Joseph Exaudet.

In describing the young Saint-Georges at that time, which was later maintained by those who knew him and his parents, it was said that he combined the grace and features of his beautiful African mother, Nanon, with the strength of Monsieur de Boulogne. The young boy's vigor was highly pleasing to his father, who frequently chuckled and said he thought he had produced a man. But, in fact he had fathered a sparrow, so quick, observant and lively were the movements of the boy. This sparrow was to grow into an eagle and soar into the highest realms of achievement. It was said very early on of Saint-Georges that no young man united so much suppleness to so much strength. He excelled in all the bodily exercises in which he engaged; he was an excellent swimmer and skater to begin with. There were many more accomplishments to come from the Chevalier de Saint-Georges.

Saint-Georges, as a young boy of ten, sailed to Paris in 1749 with his father. By that time he had amazed his tutors with his ability to learn. His mother did not accompany them on this voyage but settled in Paris at a later date given as 1760. By the time Saint-Georges had reached the age of twelve in 1751, he took part in his first fencing match – the first recorded – against L'Ouverture Breda. The exceptional showing by his son encouraged Joseph Boulogne to place him en pension at the age of thirteen with the celebrated fencing master, La Boessiere, then aged twenty-nine. Saint-Georges spent his mornings doing the traditional studies of music, literature, science and mathematics; in the afternoons he went through fencing and boxing exercises. Coming from the islands he had already mastered the technique of swimming. Added to these, he became an expert at shooting, skating, riding and dancing. In fact, it can safely be claimed that there was nothing that the amazing Saint-Georges put his mind and his hands and feet to that he could not do, and do with the ease and expertise of the professional. Saint-Georges finished his fencing studies with La Boessiere in 1758, and in the following year he defeated the invincible Picard – considered the best in France. For that achievement, his father presented Saint-Georges with a small white horse and a cabriolet.

Among some of the fantastic physical feats performed by Saint-Georges was to frequently swim over the river Seine in Paris with one arm, and to surpass others by his skating ability upon that river's surface in the covered winter months. He was an equestrian of note and a remarkable shot with pistols and guns, using either hand. Henry Angelo, a friend and fencer whose father, Domenico Angelo, ran a fencing academy in London, noted about Saint-Georges' myriad attainments as a friend and fencer:

> His talents in music unfolded themselves rapidly; but the art in which he surpassed all his contemporaries and predecessors, was fencing; no professor or amateur ever showed so much accuracy, such strength, such length of lunge, and such quickness. His attacks were a perpetual series of hits; his parade was so close that it was in vain to attempt to touch him–in short, he was all nerve.

Saint-Georges suffered his first tragedy at the age of twenty-one. Soon after the year 1760 his father, Boulogne père died. The young son who had just reached his manhood was deeply grieved at the passing of his father. Boulogne père loved and adored his outstanding son. In leaving a large portion of his substantial estate to Saint-Georges he also included his son's mother, Nanon, and a daughter, Elizabeth Benedictine de Boulogne, whose mother was another African woman from the Caribbean. Saint-Georges' father was a respected and honored French gentleman in spite of his clandestine affairs with African women, and so the Rue Boulogne in Guadeloupe was named after him. Ironically enough, on 28 November 1912, the government of that island re-christened that same street Rue du Chevalier-Saint-Georges.

The year after his father's death, honors began to come Saint-Georges' way and he was appointed a member of the Royal Guard in 1761, serving the Duke of Chartres.

Saint-Georges, needless to say, cut a dashing romantic figure. The ladies found him irresistible and naturally their boudoir doors were flung wide open for him. He was made very welcome with embracing arms. Society buzzed with stories about his fencing matches, lady killing, suppers and gallant adventures. He began to spend a little too liberally sums from the 8,000 pounds his father left him. He threw money around without giving it a thought, led a life in the lap of luxury; and it was not until about 1770, when he was thirty-one years old, that he appears to have begun to think of music seriously, that is, as a composer. Prior to 1766 he had studied music assiduously for several years under Jean-Marie Leclair and François Gossec, two very famous teachers. Of the two music teachers it was Gossec who turned out to be more important in Saint-Georges' life as a musician. The Belgian composer had played a very active part in musical circles in Paris since 1751 and had previously been conductor of the famous concerts given by Le Riche de La Poupliniere, the tax farmer. Gossec was then appointed director to the court of the Prince de Conde in 1763. It was during this period that he taught Saint-Georges. Gossec thought so highly of his unusual and talented student that he dedicated to Saint-Georges his six string trios, *Opus 9*, with this laudatory note accompanying them:

> To Monsieur de Saint-Georges, Chevalier, member
> of the Royal Guard.
> Monsieur,
>
> The celebrated reputation which you have given
> to artists encourages me to take the liberty of
> dedicating these works to you, as an homage
> merited by a brilliant amateur. With your approval,
> their success is certain. I am, with respect Monsieur,
> your very humble servant.
>
> F.-J. Gossec, of Anvers

This kind of admiration shows the high esteem in which a master held a brilliant pupil. But Gossec was not the only man of such stature to shower Saint-Georges with these feelings of praise. Antonio Lolli graciously presented him with his two pairs of violin concertos (Op 2 and 4) and signed to this, "Gendarme de la Gard de Sa Majeste." Another dedication was made by Karl Stamitz (his Op. 1 set of string quartets); and yet one more from J. Avolio (his Op. 4 set of six violin sonatas, published by Breitkopf). These manifestations of admiration for the musical talents of Saint-Georges were certainly not ill bestowed. He went on to climb loftier heights of glory. Later on, Talleyrand, Napoleon's powerful chancellor, stated that Saint-Georges was "the most accomplished human being he had ever met." Saint-Georges' only defect–and it was a minor one–was that he stammered slightly.

During the time when Gossec published his Trios, dedicated to Saint-Georges, and dated 1766, the gifted African was living a life of comfort and ease receiving an annuity of 8,000 lires from his father's estate. This was quite a sizable allowance compared to the salary of 2,000, Mozart was offered twelve years later as an organist at the Palace of Versailles. Through his talents Saint-George gained much popularity and recognition from the highest circles. Titled persons and royalty fell under his charms. At age twenty he was appointed Esquire to the Duchess of Orleans, wife of the brother of Louis XVI. He was also a confidant of the Duke himself and of his son, the Duke of Chartres. All these contacts led him into the whirl of the exciting court life at Versailles where, in the words of a historian, "his physical charm, his talents, and his taste in dress made him the most striking figure in that scintillating throng."

One of the amazing facets of this amazing African was that he could find the time and occasions to display his variety of talents. He was equally at home with the rapier, the bow or the baton. For instance, around the time that Gossec was dedicating trios to the violinist-composer, Saint-Georges would indulge in fencing matches. One such match was with the Italian master of the sword from Pisa, named Guiseppe "Faldoni" Gianfaldoni. He had conquered all French opponents and asked for a match with Saint-Georges. The French wanted to see the match, and for the honor of France the Black Chevalier accepted the contest. It took place on 8 September 1766. The outcome of the match remains in doubt. Faldoni, in a letter to his father the next day, claimed to have won four out of six thrusts, adding that he doubted Saint-Georges had an equal in France. Other references to this match gave the decision in Saint-Georges' favor. J.A. Rogers, in his writings on Saint-Georges, commented thus: "When only twenty-one he (Saint-Georges) defeated Faldoni, the renowned fencing champion of Italy." There were many other fencing victories.

The Chevalier's successes with the sword made him a man of distinction, moving in the best circles in the land by virtue also, of his high position in King's Guard. His life during that period was described by his contemporaries as one of "fencing matches, lady-killing, suppers and gallant adventures." Saint-Georges spent his money without a thought for the morrow, and kept on with his life of luxury. It was not until 1770, when Saint-Georges was thirty-one, that he began to think seriously about music, although his first compositions – six string quartets – had been published in 1765, and notice began to be taken of his musical talents. During the winter months of 1772-73, the season of concerts by the famous Concert des Amateurs, then the rage of all Paris, began with a bang. The reason for that was that two concertos for violin and orchestra, by Saint-Georges, were being played by none other than the violinist-composer himself. In the words of the writer-critic John Duncan: "These concerts acquired a decided popularity for a time even though they were his first serious efforts in composition."

This was a high point in the exciting life of the Chevalier de Saint-Georges, mainly because the Concerts des Amateurs was under the baton of the great Gossec. This famous orchestra occupied a place of honor in the history of music at that time and for all time.

The violin virtuosity of the Chevalier had tongues busy singing his praises. In his *Les Maitres Classiques du Violin,* Delphin Alard wrote, "Although he developed as an amateur he became the best French violinist of his time." Saint-Georges' bravura style captivated all who heard him. His most effective and spectacular playing was when he handled very rapid passages to the highest notes of the instrument and then dropped immediately to a low full tone. Violinists of the time were not capable of such dexterity and prowess with the bow. The story is told by those who witnessed the incident that one evening, Saint-Georges played a piece of music on his violin with a whip. This whip became famous, and the handle was ornamented with a large number of precious stones; each stone in the dazzling collection represented a woman who had fallen in love with Saint-Georges.

From pinnacle to pinnacle this extraordinary musician-composer ascended. In June of 1773, the music publisher Sieber issued six quartets by Saint-Georges. They were dedicated to the Prince de Robecq. This established an important fact in musical circles: that Saint-Georges and Gossec were the first French musicians to write string quartets. In that very year Gossec gave up the leadership of Concerts des Amateurs and the baton was passed on to Chevalier de Saint-Georges. Audiences applauded him loudly and long whenever he appeared on the rostrum and played his compositions. His works were en vogue and admirers followed this magnificent African wherever and whenever he was performing. In the years that followed this gifted man created works in rapid succession. The year 1775 was certainly his most productive year. In June of that year the French publisher, Bailleux, presented to the public a set of four violin concertos by Saint-Georges. By that December Saint-Georges had produced a collection of simphonies concertantes, one of which was played at the Concert Spiritual on Christmas Day. Incidentally, it was in 1773 that Gossec left the Concert des Amateurs for the Concert Spiritual just mentioned, and so named because the concerts were given on Sundays. The vacancy created by Gossec was filled by Saint-Georges who, in the words of Professor Dominique-Rene De Lerma, "continued to play first violin and conducted, when the ensemble needed such assistance, with a baton, his bow, a roll of paper, or by tapping his foot, according to the custom."

More good things happened to the Chevalier de Saint-Georges in the field of music when he received an undertaking from Bailleux to have his works published for the next six years. His production flowed steadily. For the following fifteen years Saint-Georges was to play an ever-increasing and important part in Parisian musical life. Today, he seems to have faded in the night behind Bach, Haydn, Mozart and Beethoven. But in his heyday, in those latter years of the eighteenth century, it was the great African Chevalier that held the light. It was he who negotiated with Haydn on the subject of six symphonies that are known today as "Parisiennes," and which were intended for performance by Concert de la Loge Olympique.

In that busy year of 1775 Saint-Georges, who had just moved his residence to Rue Guenegaud, received an invitation to become the director of the Academie Royale de Musique (later to be named the Paris Opera). However, that was one occasion when his race was to come into question. Three of the star members of that august company conspired against Saint-Georges. Sophie Arnould, a leading soprano, joined forces with Mlles. Rosalie, another singer and Guimard, a dancer, and petitioned Queen Marie Antoinette that, "their honor and the delicacy of their conscience prevented them from accepting orders from a mulatto." When the gallant Saint-Georges heard this, though piqued, he accepted their racism with nobility and good grace and held on to his position with the Concert des Amateurs. The Opera office went to one Berton, whose caliber did not match up to that of the outstanding Chevalier. As though to make amends to Saint-Georges for the decision she made, the Queen, who had always been on the closest of terms with him – and by way of an apology – invited him to the Palais Royal to take part with her in a musical performance.

That blow to the African did not affect his stature in the eyes of the nobility. By 1777 Saint-Georges was offered and he accepted the post of Lieutenant de Chasses de Pinci, a position created for him by Mme. de Montesson. The position concerned itself more with production of theatre pieces and concerts, than with the supervision of ducal hunts. Saint-Georges became the sole controller of the Duke's theatre, in which Mme. De Montesson played the leading roles. Thus the Chevalier found himself totally involved in the social artistic and political centers of royal society. Madame de Montesson (1725-1785) was the morganatic and second wife of the Duke of Orleans, to whom she became betrothed in 1773. This morganatic marriage signified that the Duke's wife, by virtue of her lower social standing, could not be heir to her husband's estate. When the Duke died in 1785 he left as his heir Louis-Philippe-Joseph d'Orleans (1747-1793), his son-in-law, later to be known as the monarch Philippe Égalité, whose friendship with Chevalier de Saint-Georges was quite a close one.

The African composer turned his talented hands to opera and in July 1777 produced his first opera, *Ernestine*, at the Comedie Italienne. It was not a success. While the music journals of the time praised the excellence of the musical score by Saint-Georges, the libretto prepared by Captain Valmont de Choderlos de Laclos of the French artillery was, in the words of Baron von Grimm, "a masterpiece of platitude and poor taste."

Another misfortune occurred to the very popular African two years later. Obviously a victim of jealousy, Saint-Georges almost lost his life in a devilish plot. The circumstances of this intrigue have so far not been able to be established with any clarity but it seems almost certain that the assailants were the police themselves. After they failed they pleaded with the Duc d' Orleans to hush up the matter. This attempt on his life made Saint-Georges a greater figure in the French capital. His name was on all lips. Stories about his exploits were spoken everywhere. He continued with the same lifestyle, leading an expensive life, frequenting salons and boudoirs. But he also worked tirelessly and energetically producing for the Comedie, composing quartets, concertos, sinfonies concertantes, and gaining even higher success than before. Saint-Georges enjoyed his popularity to the fullest. In the winter months it was deemed one of the most thrilling sights at Versailles to witness Saint-Georges skate on the huge artificial lake. J. A. Rogers described the scene:

> Tall, lithe and graceful, he would skim over the ice with the ease of a swallow, describing marvelous rhomboids, flowers,' portraits, and sometimes "whole lines from Racine."

Saint-Georges was a prolific composer producing a variety of compositions: from string quartets to simphonies concertantes, to operas, to symphonies (Op. 11). The last named turned out, like the rest of his music, to be excellent. They were the first works in that form to be written by an African composer. The second of the symphonies was included as the overture to the only fully surviving opera by Saint-Georges, "L'Amant Anonyme." This opera was performed 8 March 1780, by Mme. de Montesson's theater devotees. Saint-Georges was now hitting his peak point as a composer and violinist, although hardly a full decade had gone by since his debut in either field of endeavor. The complete manuscript score of the successful opera "L'Amant Anonyme (The Anonymous Lover)" has been preserved in the Paris Conservatoire. Not satisfied with his host of successes, Saint-Georges turned to acting in comedy. His grace and elegance and his natural sense of theatre in its widest dimensions brought him further plaudits in that area.

A very important phase in the life of Saint-Georges was coming to a close. His last symphonie concertante (Op. 13) was published by Seiber in 1782. Then the death of his royal patron, the Duc d' Orleans, in 1785 heralded a drastic change in his fortune. He had lived lavishly and exceptionally well and his monies had dwindled and, in fact, had disappeared. Also, the four years before the Revolution, with their economic and political unrest, had posed many problems to the French aristocracy. When Saint-Georges worked for Mme. de Montesson in 1777, he lived on Rue de Provenance. Later, he moved to Chausee d'Antin. It was from this location that he left for London to resume his career as a fencer.

From 1786-1787 Saint-Georges took his first trip to London, where he was accorded a hero's welcome. The entire English aristocracy received the Chevalier royally. One of the most noteworthy fencing matches of the century took place there on 9 April 1787 at Carlton House, in the presence of the Prince of Wales and many members of the British nobility. The fencers taking part included Fabien, Nagee, Reda, Rolland and Goddard. Saint-Georges partner for this event was the Chevalier d'Eon (full name: Charles-Genevieve-Louise-August-Andre-Timothee, Chevalier d'Eon de Beaumont). He wore women's clothes all the time and used the name Chevalier d'Eon. He was then sixty, fully ten years older than Saint-Georges. As was expected, the African was the victor. It has been said that his match against this bisexual opponent was the inspiration for a comic opera called *La Fille Garcon*, produced in Paris at the

Comedie Italienne on 18 August 1788.

While in London, Henry Angelo, the son of fencing master Domenico Angelo, made friends with Chevalier de Saint-Georges, The two swordsmen became very close, so much so that Angelo commissioned Mather Brown, the American pupil of Benjamin West, to paint a half-length portrait of the Chevalier. Saint-Georges himself said the picture "Si ressemblant que c'etait affreux." There exists a fine colored engraving of this portrait. The picture itself, once most highly treasured by Henry Angelo, adorned the Angelo School of Arms for about a century.

The Chevalier de Saint-Georges made yet another trip to London, leaving behind in Paris his friends the Baron de Besenval and Dalayrac. The year was 1789, the year of the French Revolution, and Saint-Georges was accompanying the new Duke of Orleans, an ardent liberal who became known as Philippe Égalité after the fall of the monarchy in 1792. The relationship was a political one, though Saint-Georges' main preoccupations in London were fencing and living the life of a lavish host at Grenier's Hotel. However, Saint-Georges sought consort with many supporters of the French Revolution and liberal causes. This was not at all surprising since royalty looked at Blacks and those from the colonies with even less tolerance than it did the French native peasants.

The Duke's trip to London was one of exile. Historians claim that the Duke used Saint-Georges to further his political ends. In company with his companion Louise Fusil and the horn player Lamothe, Saint-Georges was ordered out of several French towns even though Louise Fusil claimed that their mission was purely for concert purposes. City officials believed otherwise. At one place the reason given for his non-acceptance was that refugees did not like his liberal views. Others maintained that it was his reputation of accepting patronage from royalty, which prompted them to distrust him. His movements during those dangerous years 1789 to 1791 are hidden in a measure of secrecy. What is certain is that Saint-Georges was back in Paris in 1790 for the performance of his last opera, *Guillaume Tout Coeur* (Unfortunately the score for this significant work cannot be traced anywhere).

The French Revolution was now in full swing. Saint-Georges, by June 1791, thought it prudent to live in Tournai, a city of refuge for nobles and under Austrian control. The African did not hide his liberal sentiments and his leanings towards the revolutionaries. Consequently, he was not a popular figure in that city. But the city of Lille welcomed him with open arms, and appointed him Captain of the city's National Guard division. The versatile African could even find time in these dangerous days to take part in a concert on 3 November in a program that consisted of one of his sonatas for two unaccompanied violins. During those late years his closest friends were the actress Louise Fusil and the hornist Lamothe.

On 24 March 1792, France passed a law making it legal for Blacks to "verser leur sang pour la defense de la patrie," and between 8 and 15 September an all-Black regiment called Legion Nationale des Americans et du Midi was formed. It consisted of 800 Infantrymen, to which were added 200 horsemen, known as Hussards Americans et du Midi, on 6 December. The eight troops which made up the thirteenth regiment were popularly referred to as the Legion des Hommes du Couleur, or the Legion Saint-Georges. who had been chosen as its Colonel. The soliders of this regiment were Blacks, former slaves from the French Caribbean territories and now residents of Bordeaux. Included in that regiment was someone who was to be a future general, the Marquis Dumas Davy de la Pailleterie, whose son was to become the celebrated man of letters, Alexandre Dumas, pére.

Colonel Saint-Georges was now serving in the regiment under the command of General Dumourier. The General envied the success and popularity of the Chevalier and was not on very friendly terms with him, even though he had also been a member of the Orleans circle. Problems between the two began to surface on 2 May 1793, when Commissioner Dufrene expressed the belief that Saint-Georges had siphoned off regimental funds to pay for his personal debts. Saint-Georges left Lille to go to Paris on 25 June to stand trial. He was found guilty and dismissed from the service on 25 September. At first he was detained at Haudainville and then, in October, he was sent to Clermont-sur-Oise, where he remained for one year. All his objections and answers to those charges proved fruitless. However, officials were forced to look again at the evidence and arrived at the conclusions that his removal was nothing less than an arbitrary measure, as unjust as it was unjustified. Consequently, the Committee of Public Safety examined the case report again and, on the strength of their findings this time, the Committee was faced with an alternative: to reinstate Saint-Georges in command of the American Hussars. This the Committee did on the 24th Floreal in the year III; that is, the eighth month of the calendar of the first French republic. During 1793, the Legion Saint-Georges, as the Hussars were sometimes referred to, was active against the hostilities in Amiens, then in Laon, before being called to the campaign in Belgium. Reports stated that the regiment with Saint-Georges as Chief of Brigade over the Black soldiers performed brilliantly throughout the operations. Some of his enemies stated that he plunged his troops head on into battle and suffered heavy losses. Yet most of his compatriots gave him the highest praise for his maneuvers in battle. He remained in command thereafter for another year. His patriotism was praiseworthy said one of his military colleagues "even though his military ability was intuitive."

Colonel Saint-Georges' command continued until 1795. However, disillusioned and unhappy over the treatment he had received even though his good name had been cleared, he resigned his post on 29 October. Very soon after that he left Bordeaux to return to Saint Dominique accompanied by M. Raymond, an early supporter for the establishment of an all-Black regiment, and himself a native of Hispaniola. The two men plunged themselves into the fierce revolution taking place between the wealthy landowners, both French and Spanish, and the Africans enslaved on that island. Saint-Georges, in spite of all the luxury and adulation he had enjoyed in royal circles in France, quickly turned to his African people, his mother's people, his people when his loyalty and help were most required. Fighting in support of his people in Saint Dominique almost cost him his life when he narrowly escaped hanging.

Physically, Saint-Georges was exceptionally active until he was forty years old. At that age he was forced to cut down on some of his more strenuous activities, particularly fencing, having damaged his Achilles heel while dancing in 1779. While one aspect of his fantastic life has been brought to the fore, that of his adulation by Parisian society for his physical charms, elegance and many accomplishments, it must not be imagined that Saint-Georges was not very conscious of his African background. As one writer commented:

> His nobility of character never shone brighter than in the manner in which he received his humble mother, once a slave, when she came to Paris. Taking her into the most brilliant salons, he presented her to his aristocratic friends, letting it quietly be known that whoever attempted to snub her would in turn be snubbed by him. "Who refuses her, refuses me," he said.

Although his color gave him a certain exoticism, and the ladies of both London and Paris worshipped him, that in itself was enough to cause some outrage among men and incite jealous attempts to do evil to the African. He suffered, quite apart from the intrigue which cast a small shadow (later removed) on his military career, petty insults and snubs, some already noted in this study. There was the occasion, too, while walking on the Rue de Bac, a pedestrian tried to be funny and shouted the word "moricaud," the French equivalent of "darky," at the African. Saint-Georges seized the man, rubbed his face in the muddy gutter, and jestingly remarked, "There you are now! As black as I am!"

On yet another occasion Saint-Georges was snubbed because of his color and illegitimacy. He was asked by the Duke of Orleans to call on a group of *émigrés*, discontented nobles who had left the court. They refused point-blank to be seen by this African, as talented and noble and as popular as he was in Parisian circles. It was claimed then that it was because of the queen's support of color discrimination that sent him to the ranks of the republicans. It was also said that he was inducted into republicanism by the Duke of Orleans, Philippe Égalité. However, both claims are wrong, if the correspondence of Saint-Georges is examined. His papers conclude that he was a democrat at heart even though he was reared as and lived the life of an aristocrat. Saint-Georges did not hesitate to say in words and to prove by his actions during the revolutions in France, that he was a an African born among his enslaved peoples and that his sympathies, which had always been with them, would remain so.

It is this quality in this remarkable man's life that has escaped the pens of chroniclers, very few in number as they are. Like another African giant, Alexandre Dumas, péré, Saint-Georges was generous to a fault and up to the time of his death he had a list of pensioners whom he supported from his private purse, even in his most lean times. Larousse wrote of Saint-Georges: "He distinguished himself among the personages of his time...by a generosity and a rectitude of character very rare. To the end of his days he did good."

In that respect the views of his contemporaries were unanimous: that he was a man full of generosity and delicacy and feeling. Liberal and benevolent, he repeatedly deprived himself of the necessities of life in order to aid those who were unfortunate. It was agreed by all who came into contact with this remarkable man that at all times, he acted "as a philanthropist to the aged and ill."

There were those of his times who said that when he returned to Paris from his war experience in Saint Dominique fighting with the forces of Toussaint L'Ouverture, he resumed the old life of a Bohemian. To be more exact, he took up his activities as a musician. There in Paris, he led the Circle d'Harmonie, "an exclusive, socially oriented group which met in the former home of the Duke of Orleans." At that time he was living in a modest apartment in the Marais District. The life he led had been a hectic one and his health collapsed. Attended by a neighbor and former regimental officer named Nicholas Duhamel, Saint-Georges succumbed to what was at the time described as an ulcerous bladder, and he died on June 10, 1799. He had reached the age of 60.

Many were the obituaries of praise that were showered on this most remarkable personality. Beauvoir paid tribute to him, calling him this "brilliant mulatto, this man of combat, of good fortunes and of sighs, this unique man." La Laurencie recorded that "just as Watteau and Boucher were basic representatives of eighteenth-century France, so was Saint-Georges, who gave us pictures in sound, both impressive and green, from a soul as lively and nuanced as the period itself." French writer Joel-Marie Fauquet said that:

Certain of his friends declared that the walls of his alcove were covered with women's letters, reminders of a brilliant past with he frequently reviled! It was at this moment that this most gifted and seductive personality, who scorned wealth and considered that his possessions belonged to others, died on June 10th, 1799, above all faithful to Music. The Chevalier de Saint-Georges showed in his life-time that he was a man of many talents, with but a single passion: Music."

Dominique-Rene De Lerma, Professor of Music at Morgan State University, once wrote that:

"It does everyone a great injustice to refer to Saint-Georges as a "Black Mozart" or a "Black Haydn." What Saint-Georges had in common with these two, he had in common with other composers of his time from all over Europe. It is the thing he possessed that was different that matters."

What is of greater significance here is the gross injustice that this comparison has done to Saint-Georges more than anyone else. It was not Saint-Georges who was influenced but Mozart and Haydn. Joel-Marie Fauquet makes this point quite clearly:

In order to establish the truth, it must be stated that Saint-Georges remains, it is too often forgotten today, one of the principal exponents of the French style of the sinfonia concertante and the violin concerto, and it was on the contrary Mozart, with his extraordinary genius for integrated new ideas, who introduced the quintessence of what he learned form the Parisian violinists influenced by the Mannheim school, into his own violin concertos. The circumstances were those of this second visit to Paris in 1788.

One final comment on this comparison of Saint-Georges, Mozart, and Haydn was made by De Serma when he concluded:

> Aside from the impropriety of describing a musician in racial terms, to call Saint-Georges a "Black Mozart" or a "Black Haydn" betrays an ignorance both of French music and of Haydn and Mozart.

And, most importantly, of Saint-Georges! That he was of African origin whose mother had been enslaved on a Caribbean island makes the story of the Chevalier de Saint-Georges one of the great epics of African achievement of all times. There are countless stories of this magnitude which have remained untold and entombed in the archives of European and North American libraries and museums.

This study of Saint-Georges has been subtitled: Composer, Conductor, Violinist, Swordsman, Equestrian, Soldier. Make no mistake, this African genius was a man of many talents with many strings to his bow. He did them all with superhuman brilliance, excelling at all. A poet of his times paid homage to him with these lines:

> His equal was never seen in fencing,
> Charming musician, facile composer.
> Swimming, skating, hunting, horseback riding
> All exercise was ultimately easy for him
> And in each he found his own style.
> If so much modesty is joined to these talents
> Of this incomparable French Hercules
> It is that his good spirit, free from jealousy,
> Has found that kindness in this short life
> From his good friends and warm heart

There is no doubt that the poet who wrote these lines in praise of the Chevalier, calling him "this incomparable French

Hercules" meant well, and very well, indeed. But there is no doubt that Africans on the Motherland and in the Diaspora would prefer instead to liken Saint-Georges to another African of myriad talents, and call him the AFRICAN IMHOTEP.

REFERENCES

Angelo, Henry, *Angelo's Picnic or Table Talk*, pp. 21-5 (London: John Ebbers, 1834)

Angelo, Henry, *Reminiscences, Vol. II*, pp. 308-9, 398, 421 (London, 1834)

Beauvoir, Eugene, *La Chevalier De Saint-Georges* (Paris, 1806-66.)

Biographies from Tuesday Magazine, *Le Chevalier de Saint-Georges*, pp. 60-7, (New York, Toronto, London: Bantam Pathfinder Edition, 1966, 1967, 1968)

De Lerma, Dominique-Rene, "The Chevalier de Saint-Georges," *Revista/Review Interamericana*, Vol. VIII, No. 4, Winter 1978-9

_____, "The Chevalier de Saint-Georges," *The Black Perspective in Music* (Fall 1985, Vol. 13, No. 2)

Duncan, John, "The Chevalier de Saint-Georges: Musician-Patriot," *Negro History Bulletin* (March 1946), pp. 129-30, 142. *Association for the Study of Negro Life and History*, Washington, DC

_____, *The Negro Literary Influence on Masterpieces of Music* pp. 134-7 (March 1958) Washington, DC

Duveyrier, Anne, "Le Chevalier de Saint-Georges,"
1787-1865, Henahan, Donal, *The Composer as Musketeer*,
New York Times, January 24, 1982

Scobie, Edward, *Black Britannia,*
(Chicago: Johnson Publishing Company, 1972)

CHAPTER SEVEN

The Caribbean and the American Revolution

In the eighteenth century, British North America and, later, the islands of the British West Indies, had one thing in common: they were colonies of Great Britain at that time ruled by the Hanoverian Georges—George I, George II, and most important of the three as far as the American Revolution was concerned, George III (1760-1820). But it was British North America that was the first to free itself from the colonial domination of Britain. However, the affairs, and indeed, the fortunes of the two wide geographical areas (one a continent, the other a string of islands in the Caribbean Sea) were inextricably woven into each other. The effects of the American Revolution were felt no less in America than in the British West Indies; in fact, in every territory of the Caribbean, British or otherwise.

To be able to examine this previous statement, it is necessary to give a clear picture of the conditions between continental America and the Caribbean at the time leading up to the American Revolution. On the eve of the Revolution, after Boston Harbor had been closed, American minister John Adams observed in the light of the West Indian Trade that "it was an essential link in a vast chain, which has made New England what it is, the Southern provinces what they are, the West Indian islands what they are." In actual fact, the trade not only with the British islands, but with all the Caribbean islands, had become the cornerstone of the American economy long before the colonies had risen in revolt. And, Adams realized this quite clearly when he said "our trade could not be taken from us, or granted stingily, and rendering without tearing."

This statement by Adams was no exaggeration. In 1770, the continental colonies shipped to the Caribbean nearly one-third of their exports of dried fish and almost all their pickled fish; seven-eights of their flour; all their butter and cheese; over one-quarter of their rice, almost all their onions; five-sixths of their pine, oak, and cedar boards, over half of their stayes, nearly all of their hoops, all their horses, sheep, hogs and poultry; almost all their soap and candles. In the words of Professor Frank Pitman: "It was the wealth accumulated from West Indian trade which more than anything else underlay the prosperity and civilization of New England and the Middle Colonies."

In the imperial policy of Britain in the eighteenth century, the mainland colonies came second to the West Indies. To quote historian Dr. Eric Williams:

> Sugar was king, and the West Indian islands the sugar bowl of Europe.
>
> The acquisition of Jamaica made Cromwell so happy that he refused to transact any further business on the day when the glad tidings were announced. He would have taken a week's holiday if he had captured Hispanola, the French part of which, Saint Dominique, later became the pearl of the Antilles and the bane of the British planters. Barbados was the "fair jewell" of His Majesty's Crown, a little pearl more precious and rare than any the Kings of Europe possessed, and in 1661 Charles II showed its importance by creating thirteen baronets among its planters in a single day. The governor-ship of Jamaica ranked next in colonial appointments to the lord-lieutenancy

of Ireland, and the postal system made better provision for the islands than for the mainland.

The mercantilists looked with foreboding at the northern colonies in particular. They saw that the latter were plentiful in farmers, merchants, fishermen, and seamen, but no planters. They concluded that these colonies in the North were, with the exception of their yet undeveloped manufacturers, in a very literal sense, "New England." And a rivalry with Old England was bound to take place. They competed with Britain in the fisheries, which became a nursery for the seamen of New England. In their agricultural products they could, by virtue of their situation, undersell their British rivals in island markets. By this competition Britain was losing, in sales and freights, two-and-a-half million Sterling a year. An anonymous writer of the time posed the question: "Can any one think from hence that the trade and navigation of our colonies are worth one grout to this nation?" And Sir Josiah Child made this observation "that ten men in Massachusetts did not provide employment for a single Englishman at home." He concluded: "New England is the most prejudicial plantation to this kingdom." A general prejudice against the mainland colonies was felt by both English planters and parliamentarians. Chichester said that he "would have preferred to labor with his hands in Ireland than 'dance and sing in Virginia.'" Petty exclaimed bluntly that, "the inhabitants of New England should be repatriated or sent back to Ireland." Attempts were initiated to persuade new Englanders to immigrate to the Bahamas, to Trinidad, to Maryland, and to Virginia. Oliver Cromwell, England's Lord Protector during the interregnum period of the Commonwealth, viewed New England with "only an eye of pity, as poor, cold and useless." In 1655 the governors and inhabitants were instructed to make offers to go to Jamaica "to enlighten those parts...by the people who know and fear the Lord; that those of New England, driven from the land of their nativity into that desert and barren wilderness, for conscience sake may remove to a land of plenty."

These attitudes were obviously too extreme. To begin with, if the Northern colonies were pushed out of the provisions trade, they would quite understandably be unable to pay for British manufactures; and these exports were "more valuable to England that the export of agricultural commodities and salted meat." What was infinitely worse to the British was that the colonists might prefer to "develop their own industries." Better than that the northern colonists should control the food trade, argued Charles Davenant, one of the ablest economists and financial experts of his day.

Davenant, like other British men of importance and power, knew full well that the West Indian colonies needed food. If they were to depend on the sugar to which the economic strictures of the mercantile era confined them, they had no other place where staples could be obtained. Also, "their cash crop was too profitable for them to afford the luxury of diverting land and labor to cattle grazing and food crops." A resident informed Governor Winthrop in 1647 about the West Indies that "Men are so intent upon planting sugar that they had rather buy foode at very deare rates than produce it by labour, so infinite is the profit of sugar workes after once accomplished." Thus the tradition was set by which sugar became "the wheat or bread of the West Indies." The conclusion was that "only the possession of the mainland colonies permitted this sugar monopoly of the West Indian soil."

Thus, in that manner, the North American colonies became an integral part in the imperial economy, as suppliers of commodities required by the sugar planters and their slaves. The New Englanders were looked upon as the Dutchman of America. The mainland colonies, mainly the New England and mid-Atlantic ones, produced not "only food, but horses to provide the motive power of the tread-mills used in sugar manufacture, and lumber for buildings that were the articles most in demand in the islands." Samuel Vetch wrote in 1708:

> There is no island the British possess in the West
> Indies that is capable of subsisting without the
> assistance of the Continent, for to them we transport
> their bread, drink and all the necessaries of humane
> life, their cattle and horses for cultivating their
> plantations, lumber and staves of all sorts to make
> casks for their rum, sugar and molasses, without
> which they could have none, ships to transport their
> goods to the European markets, nay, in short, their
> very houses they inhabit are carried over in frames,
> together with shingles that cover them, in so much
> that their well being, depend almost entirely upon
> the Continent.

Planters on the islands knew the value of commodities they received from the mainland. A Boston factor wrote in 1674:

> The Barbadians are all sensible of the great
> prejudice which will accrue to them for they loose
> the benefit of those two commodities, which are
> vendable in no part of the world but New England
> and Virginia.

This practice of dependence was deliberately planned by the statesmen of England and the planters in the colonies. Many of the commodities exported by New England to the West Indies could have been produced in the islands. A Jamaican planter there questioned, "If this island were able to maintain itself with diet and other necessaries what would become of the New England trade?" Obviously, the answer is that without the sugar islands the mainland colonies would have been seriously hampered. The mainland became "the key to the Indies." Without that, Eric Williams contended, "the islands would have been unable to feed themselves except by a diversion of profitable sugar land to food crops, to the detriment not only of New England farmers but British shipping, British refining, and the customs revenue, glory, and grandeur of England."

Williams added that:

> Economic relations between the islands and mainland were further strengthened by individual contacts. West Indians owned property on the mainland. North Americans owned plantations in the islands. The Middletons, Bulls and Colletons of South Carolina owned plantations in Jamaica and Barbados. Aaron Lopez, a Rhode Island slave trader, was owner of a sugar plantation in Antigua. Alexander Hamilton was born in Nevis. The Gedney Clarkes of Salem are the outstanding example of North American success in the islands. The father owned extensive plantations in Barbados and Guiana. His son became surveyor general of customs in Barbados, member of the House of Assembly and subsequently of the Council. North Americans soon discovered the value of West Indian sunshine. West Indians sought in North America the recovery of broken constitutions…West Indian heiresses, it is said, were as desirable in North America as they were in England.

For their goods and products, the mainland colonists exchanged sugar, rum and molasses from the islands in such bulk that by 1676, the English merchants were contending that "New England was becoming the great mart and staple of colonial produce;" it was a case of mutual independence between the two units. The maintenance of harmony positively demanded two conditions: island production of sugar and molasses must be sufficient to meet the demands of mainland consumption; and secondly, that island consumption of mainland staples must of necessity keep pace with mainland production.This was difficult since there were big differences in the sizes of the two areas. Thus a pull between them began.

146

Trade with the West Indies before the Revolution did not end with the Declaration of Independence. It was aggravated by years of war. The presence of the West Indies was important after the war as the United States made efforts to regain its relations with England and Europe. With American ministers Frankling, Adams and Jay pressed strongly to gain for America a portion of the carrying-trade to the West Indies when the Treaty of Paris was being drafted in 1783. Adams reported: "The West India commerce now gives us the most anxiety." Adams and his colleagues were annoyed when they did not obtain the right to allow US ships to enter British ports. He countered testily "they think America may have what she desires except a free trade with the West India Islands." Then he added: "Our natural share of the West India trade is all that is wanting to complete the plan of happiness and prosperity in our country." When the Republic was founded, Washington wrote to Governor Morris that "let it be strongly impressed on your mind, that the privilege of carrying our productions in our vessels to the West Indies and of bringing in return the productions of the islands to our own ports is regarded here of the highest importance; and you will be careful not to countenance any idea of our dispensing with it in a treaty."

All during the War of Independence, Blacks, both slave and free, took part. There were many sympathizers in the Caribbean among the slaves and free people of color. Colonial Whites there sided with the mainland colonists. British stamps were publicly burned while colonists shouted for liberty.

The Jamaica Assembly framed a petition in December 1774, while proclaiming a conventional loyalty, stated that it was, in the words of Eric Williams, "an established principle that no part of His Majesty's dominions could legislate or any other part, and that no law could bind Englishmen which had not received the assent of their representatives." The petition claimed that the British Parliament had no right to legislate for the colonies. The Jamaica Assembly agreed to abide by the commercial system, but was adamant that no laws against the interests of its constituents could be passed and imposed on them in the future. The petition declared that colonial dependence on the metropolitan country was removed when colonials did not share equal rights with Englishmen. As was to be expected the Secretary of State for the Colonies showed his annoyance publicly in England by describing the behavior of the Jamaica Assembly "indecent" and even "criminal." North Americans, quite understandably, offered votes of thanks.

Bermuda went one step further and sent delegates to the Continental Congress. The Assembly of Barbados also sympathized with the North American cause. Bahamas supported the mainland colonies. But for its navy, Britain could not prevent the British West Indies from entering the Revolution.

The effect of the American Revolution on the Caribbean was an economic one, especially on the British Caribbean territories. Williams explains in this manner:

> On the one hand, the adherence of France and Spain to the cause of the mainland colonies meant the temporary admission of American ships into the French and Spanish colonies. On the other hand the mainland ports were closed to British Caribbean produce and exports to the islands were prohibited. "God only knows," wrote a planter, "what will become of us. We must either starve or become ruined." It was worse. The British West Indies starved in the short run and were ruined in the long.

Estimates revealed that between 1780 and 1787, 15,000 slaves died of famine in Jamaica; in 1788, 100 in Antigua and about 400 in Nevis. Between March and September, 1778, over

300 Whites left St. Kitts to evade prosecution for debts. The shortage of supplies and prices rose causing Barbados to suffer greatly. The matters were even worse for Caribbean exports that had to face hostile navies and privateers.

The primary effect of the American Revolution on the West Indies, particularly on slaves, mulattoes, and other free people of color, was in actual participation in military operations. France entered in 1778, after the battle of Saratoga. Straight away, Martinique was encircled by the British fleet for four months. Reports showed that 850 men of color and 2,000 Blacks took part in that defense. The 850 men of color were counted as militia; the Blacks were servants to the troops but did take an active part in the fighting. Military regulations on the island in 1778 ordered that thirty Blacks would serve each battalion "to carry their tents, their food, their utensils, to make their soup, to cut wood, to build their cabins or huts."

Other French colonies in the West Indies were full of Black and mulatto troops. St. Lucia had 200 defenders, half of them men of color, in addition to the militia. Dominica issued an ordinance establishing a company of militia in each of its ten parishes. Men of color and Blacks were prominent in this company. In 1780, 400 slaves were given arms to protect the small islands. In that same year in St. Vincent 500 slaves were taken into the labor force to erect fortifications. Blacks and Caribs went about armed. Fear of attack by the British was justified as the French islands were attacked. St. Lucia was besieged as was Martinique, which had one of its plantations raided. Several slaves were captured; others escaped.

In 1778, another incident revealed the increasing role of Blacks in the Revolution. That was the expedition of 1779 against Savannah, then held by the British. A force of 800 free Blacks and mulattos drawn from the Caribbean islands served under Count Charles Hector d'Estaing, leader of the French fleet. Taking part in this expedition were Henri Christophe and others who were to distinguish themselves in later years in a revolution for the liberation of Blacks in Haiti. Among those others were Generals Beauvais, Rigaud, and Martial Besse. Describing the action, J.A. Rogers wrote,

> At Savannah they saved the Franco-American army from total disaster by covering their retreat. Later, when Martial Besse, a general in the French army in France, attempted to land at Charleston, he had to give a bond because of his color. France had to protest to ensure proper respect for him.

The fire of liberation on the mainland colonies had swept across the Caribbean and the Blacks got caught up in it. Bouillé, Governor General in Martinique, had written in November 1777 to the Minister of the Marine, stating that feelings among Blacks were for war. White colonists were of the same mood. Everyone was of the opinion that war was approaching and wished to take part in it. Two companies of free men of color, about 200, volunteered to serve without pay. Bouillé claimed that the number of men of color in the island was 1,000, all well armed, well dressed, well trained, and ready for battle. In the French colonies, Blacks and mulattoes made up a sizeable proportion of the colonial forces. They took part in all the engagements.

Involved in a personal way in the Revolution was one of the most important Blacks from the West Indies named Samuel Fraunces, affectionately known as Black Sam. He owned one of the finest hostelries in colonial America that catered to high society. Washington and his staff ate there regularly. Fraunces was a true patriot. The English once fired a shot from a warship in the New York harbor that crashed into his tavern. When troops were needed in New York, he was the first to enlist as a private. Washington and his officers laid their plans at his hostelry and it was from there that the Sons of Liberty plotted the dumping of the cases of East India tea into the Hudson. He helped with food and money. Officers who could not afford to pay were fed free. After the war Congress thanked him warmly and gave him a large sum. Washington said of Fraunces: "You gave invariably through the most trying times, maintained a constant friendship and attention to the cause of our country and its independence and freedom."

It was Fraunces' daughter, Phoebe, who saved Washington's life. In Washington's bodyguard was an Irishman named Hickey, an agent of the British, sent there to kill Washington. Hickey began by making love to Phoebe, who used to wait on Washington. He poisoned a dish of peas to be served to the General. Phoebe found out and warned Washington, who threw the peas out of the window to the chickens. When the chickens ate them they fell dead. Hickey was hanged while a big crowd looked on.

At the end of the American Revolution Blacks in large numbers sailed to Nova Scotia, England, Sierra Leone and the Caribbean. It is one of the paradoxes of history that thousands of Blacks did not want to remain in the new republic, which had just won its liberation from imperial Britain. Many from the southern states found the West Indies to be, at least, the most convenient stepping-stone to freedom, including the freedom of Spanish control in the Floridas. Slaves fleeing America sought refuge mainly in the Bahamas and Jamaica, both British colonies. The felt that they had better chances of decent treatment in those islands than in the hands of the colonists of the thirteen states they had just fought for victoriously for their own liberation. Over 3,000 Blacks settled in the Bahamas. The Crown of Britain provided not only transportation but also 20 acres of land to each Black and this land "to be delivered free and exempted from the burden of quit rents for ten years." In the evacuation of Savannah, 5,000 Blacks and 400 White families, sailed to Jamaica. When, in

December 1782, Charleston surrendered to the Americans, 3,891 persons set sail for Jamaica. Of that number, there were 1,278 Whites and 2,613 Blacks. At that same time, 20 Whites and 350 Blacks went to St. Lucia. These facts help to explain the remarkable increase in the population of Jamaica between the years 1775 and 1787. In 1775, the population was 18,500 Whites, 3,700 free colored people and 190, 914 slaves. The figures for 1787 stood at 30,000 Whites, 10,000 free colored and 250,000 slaves. For these slaves freedom was to come in 1834 nearly 30 years before it came for their slave brothers and sisters in the liberated republic of America.

One of the most important effects of the American Revolution was that it spurred the spirit of freedom in the hearts and minds of slaves in the Caribbean, as well as in North America, and, in fact, in the entire hemisphere. As one historian put it, "the American Revolution raised the specter of a successful independence movement" in Haiti, which became a reality in that historic August of 1791 — eight years after the end of the American Revolution. It turned out to be the first successful revolution of enslaved Africans.

REFERENCES

Cohen, David W. and Greene, Jack P., *Neither Slave Nor Free* (John Hopkins University Press, 1972).

Goveia, Elsa V., *Slave Society in the British Leeward Islands at the End of the Eighteenth Century* (Yale University Press, 1965)

McCloy, Shelby T., *The Negro in the French West Indies* (Negro Universities Press,1966.)

Rogers, J.A., *Africa's Gift To America* (Futuro Press, 1959)

Toth, Charles W., *The American Revolution and the West Indies* (Kennikat Press, 1975)

Williams, Eric, *Capitalism and Slavery* (New York: Capricorn Press, 1966)

—————, *From Columbus to Castro* (London: Andre Deustch, 1970)

CHAPTER EIGHT

Africans in the American Revolution

It is one of the tragedies of the American society that even as far back as two hundred years plus, when those fifty-six builders of the Nation had a chance of not only shouting and writing panegyrics to equality of all men, but actually turning their lofty pronouncements into reality, they failed; and failed miserably. This is not surprising since the Declaration was born of hypocrisy, of double-dealing. For, does not history tell us that Thomas Jefferson bid a fond farewell to his slaves just before he sallied forth to Philadelphia to write the Declaration of Independence? And was it not the same General Washington who fought so valiantly against the intolerable oppression of the British in the Revolutionary affair, yet who owned 300 slaves? Yes, yet another case of double standards. It is this which remains at the core of the country's national conscience, rotting it away in a manner that no anthems to liberty, no hosannas of freedom, no celebrations to an American Dream, no bicentennial charades can hide. Little wonder a slave, Prince Whipple, could utter these candid words to his master Captain William Whipple of Portsmouth, New Hampshire: "You are going to fight for your liberty but I have none to fight for."

And in England, Dr. Samuel Johnson, that literary lion of Georgian England, and no lover of the colonists, saw fit once at Oxford to pronounce on the hypocrisy of the original architects of the Dream: "Why its it we hear the loudest yelps for liberty from those who keep slaves?"

Thomas Jefferson, in an attempt to come to grips with

his conscience and to test the sincerity of his fellow colonists on the issue of slavery, included in his draft of the Declaration a stern indictment of the slave trade and slavery as one of his charges against the British monarch George III.

But Jefferson did not stop there with his accusations. He went on to charge George III of perpetuating the slave trade, and inciting the slaves to rebel against the colonists in order to gain freedom that he, the King, had taken from them! Jefferson must have been eaten up with humbug and hypocrisy not to realize that this cap fitted his colleagues perfectly. It was no wonder that these charges were removed from the final document when they proved unacceptable to the Southern delegates, including some Northerners who objected to the anti-slavery passage on the grounds that it threatened the profits they made from the slave trade. There was also the fact that some delegates thought the statement would signify the end of colonial slavery once independence had been won, and were quite obviously not prepared to pay that price. One may even concede that some delegates also realized that it was stretching the point too far beyond the bounds of belief to make Britain entirely responsible for the enslavement of Blacks by the colonists. Be that as it may, however, this was the beginning of White America's double-dealing with Blacks; and it has set a pattern that has remained constant throughout these two hundred years, and more.

Even to this advanced day there are some historians who find it difficult to understand why such reputable men could denounce the English King yet could not see inconsistency in their public statements and private lives. Jefferson made absolutely no effort to free his own slaves. He and his other Whites could have manumitted their individual slaves anytime they desired. Yet they did not. The reason was an obvious one, and it was this: as early as colonial times, the prevalent view was that Blacks were inferior and could not be classed as "men" and equals in the eyes of the Christian God. Jefferson's position was well summarized by African American historian Dr. Norman Hodges of the Department of History at Vassar College, when he wrote:

> It is indeed probable that Thomas Jefferson was a pragmatic hypocrite who sought to marshal any argument—including the issue of slavery and the slave trade—in a vigorous and emotional attack upon England that was calculated to win independence for the White colonists.

If we are to assume that the Declaration of Independence could mean whatever interpretation its signatories wanted it to mean, then the bold assumption that all men were not only "equal" but possessed certain "inalienable" rights was to turn out a permanent challenge to American racism and hypocrisy. The truth is self-evident.

History seems to delight itself in ironies; in dealing out telling blows to those who wallow in pretensions of morality. And in Boston on the fifth day of March 1770, fate dealt the colonists a resounding slap in their White faces when the first man to fall for freedom from the musket shots of the Redcoats was a Black man, Crispus Attucks! From that moment on, the white colonists were faced with one problem after another, following the unwelcome participation of quasi-free and enslaved Blacks in the Revolutionary War. It was to be the nagging question of whether they should still keep in bondage men who had aided them magnificently in their struggles for independence against the British crown. The colonists were both troubled and embarrassed by the incongruities of their dilemma and so resorted to their double game.

Right from the start of the Revolutionary War in 1775, General Washington expressed opposition to the use of Blacks in the Continental armies. In fact, it was stipulated that "any deserter from the ministerial army, nor any stroller, negro, or vagabond, or person suspected of being an enemy to the liberty of America nor any under eighteen years of age," were deemed not suitable for recruitment. In November of that year, the General quite deliberately excluded all Blacks, slave or free, from military service.

Many opinions have been voiced about Washington's edict, but the hard reality would seem that he and his generals, like Putnam, simply did not wish to have Black men armed against Whites, even though those latter were enemy solders of the infidel Hanoverian King George III. Anyway, whatever his reasons initially, the realities of forthcoming events forced Washington to undergo a change of not heart, but attitude, and play the revolutionary chess game with Black pawns on the White chess board.

What caused this was that he did not foresee that his ban on Blacks would turn out to be good news to Lord John Murray Dunmore, British governor of Virginia, who took advantage of it and made the first chess move by promising freedom and equality to all Blacks who joined him. Sir Henry Clinton, British Commander-In-Chief, had proclaimed by 1779 that all slaves in arms should be bought from their captors for the public service, and that every Black who deserted the "rebel standard" could come over to the British lines and take up any occupation he wished. These plans were, in fact, carried out. The British made efforts to organize two Black regiments in North Carolina. Between the years 1775 and 1783 the state of South Carolina lost 25,000 Blacks to the British. One-third of the soldiers garrisoned at Fort Cornwallis at the siege of Augusta were Blacks loyal to the British . There was a corps of fugitive slaves who called themselves the King of England Soldiers. For several years they harassed the people living on the Savannah River.

In the face of these happenings, the colonists loudly accused the British of starting a "race war." With their vast numbers of slaves, Southern colonists shook with fear at the consequences of the mass flight of Blacks to the royalist camps. Of this real danger Washington said: "Dunmore's strength will increase like a snowball by rolling and faster if some expedient cannot be hit upon to convince the slaves and servants of the impotency of his design." He saw that the risk of the colonists losing the war was a real one so he wrote Colonel Henry Lee on December 20, 1775. "Success will depend on which side can arm the Negroes faster." Claiming that he had learned that the Blacks who had been barred were discontented, he appealed to Congress. The latter, seeing the stark necessity of recruiting Blacks but still with an eye on appeasing the slave holders, decreed on January 16, 1776, "That the free Negroes who have served faithfully in the army at Cambridge may be re-enlisted but no others."

But the war dragged on, the ban against recruiting Blacks growing weaker and weaker. Many Whites, seeing no end to the wars, dropped out and deserted. Others sought peace with the British. General Schuyler of New York complained that when he requested more men, mostly boys and aged men were sent to him. The spirit of '76 – that same spirit that we are now glorifying—was at that time so weak that Washington complained, "The lack of patriotism is infinitely more to be dreaded than the whole forces of Great Britain assisted as they are by Hessian, Indian and Negro allies." He wrote General Laurens:

> That spirit of freedom which, at the commencement of the contest, would have gladly sacrificed everything to the attainment of its objects has long since subsided and every selfish passion has taken its place. It is not the public but private interest which influences the generality of mankind; nor can the Americans any longer boast an exception.

Under the circumstances, it would rather have
been surprising if you had succeeded nor will you,
I fear, have better luck in Georgia.

From the South, Laurens wrote Washington urging the
enlistment of Blacks as a serious necessity. He said:

The country is greatly distressed and will be so
unless reinforcements are sent to its relief. Had
we arms for 3,000 Black men as I could select in
Carolina, I should have no doubt of success in
drawing the British out of Georgia and subduing
East Florida before the end of July.

By then Blacks were accepted in such large numbers
that General Schuyler wrote: "Is it consistent with the sons of
freedom to trust their all to be defended by slaves?" In spite of
this move to recruit Black soldiers, many states in the South
wanted it both ways: to use Black men in the army yet hold
them in check as slaves. That was why Whites of these states
objected to the quota of Blacks demanded of them, especially
of Maryland. They declared it should be fixed, not on total
population, but only on the White one. Furthermore, they
feared that if White men left the colony in numbers there
would be no one to keep Blacks at bay. Accordingly, on March
14, 1779, Alexander Hamilton recommended that, "South
Carolina being very weak in her population of Whites may
be excused from the draft on condition of furnishing Black
battalions." It was decided, therefore, that South Carolina and
Georgia must take steps for raising 3,000 able-bodied Blacks.
Not unnaturally, they were to receive no pay but were given
the tenuous promise of emancipation at the end of hostilities.
It was also the common practice for White slave masters of
the South and some of the North, who did not want to risk
their lives, or those of their sons, to send Blacks to take their
place. One such Black was Samuel Charlton of New Jersey, who
fought at Monmouth and was highly recommended for his

courage, and his services in the commissary. After the war, and not surprisingly, his master refused to free him. Incidentally, the state of Virginia overruled all selfish masters and ordered Black veterans freed.

Blacks fought with valor in every theatre of the Revolutionary War. Even Prince Whipple himself, who had claimed that he had nothing to fight for, acquitted himself nobly by being one of the oarsmen who rowed George Washington across the ice-choked Delaware River in a blinding show and sleet storm on Christmas night 1776. In Washington's army, there was an average of about fifty Blacks to each battalion, and at the battle of Monmouth Courthouse in June 1778, at least 700 Blacks were on the side of the Americans. So many Black troops were raised by Massachusetts, that in 1778, it was urged that a wholly Black regiment be incorporated, but although Connecticut enlisted a separate battalion, Massachusetts continued to mix White forces. In talking about the courage of the Black soldiers, a Hessian officer, Schlozer, writing home on October 23, 1777, claimed:

> The Negro can take the field instead of his master
> and therefore no regiment is to be seen in which
> there are not Negroes in abundance and among
> them are able-bodies, strong and brave fellows.

Other observers wrote of the numbers of strong robust Blacks and mulattoes to be seen in Washington's army. In fact, Baron von Clausen says that of the 20,000 men he saw with Washington, 5,000 were Blacks. Rhode Island had a regiment composed almost entirely of slaves whose freedom had been purchased. At the battle of Rhode Island, on August 27, 1778, this regiment brought victory for its White commander, Colonel Greene, by repelling a force of 6,000 Hessian and British. Posted behind a thicket in the valley, the Black regiment three times drove back the enemy, who bore down the hill to dislodge them. The Marquis de Lafayette called this battle "the best action of the whole war."

There were Black heroes in abundance — Lexington, Concord, Bunker Hill, Brandywine, Saratoga, Monmouth, Ticonderoga, Savannah — deeds of daring by Blacks abounded. Over 5,000 Blacks fought in the ranks of the 30,000-man Continental forces. But after the war, the story was a different one, a sad one, for those Black pawns. Many were returned to slavery and lost the "promised" freedom they had so gallantly fought for. Right from this very early start, Blacks had been taken for a ride by those lovers of liberty. The pattern has remained the same. Blacks have always been fighting wars for someone else's freedom and not their own. Even after the Revolutionary War, free Blacks were forced out of the new nation's armed forces. An act of Congress in 1792 restricted service in the militia to "able-bodied White males." Blacks had to metaphorically fight their way to acceptance in American's armed forces. Slavery was later to grip the nation and pull it asunder in a war generated by the conflicts brought about by it. But that is another story.

Blacks who had been used by the British on their side, found themselves in a very sticky position at the end of the war in 1783. The majority of them had been formed into companies called Black Pioneers. At the beginning, they were mainly labor battalions, but as the war progressed they were equipped with muskets and played an active part in the fighting. Pay lists and muster rolls show that they were commanded by European officers.

By a clause in the Treaty of Paris, the British were obliged to hand back all American property. And since slaves were listed as property, the British authorities in New York — where the defeated army had assembled and was awaiting shipment to Great Britain — found themselves faced with two alternatives. They had either to break their promise to the Black Pioneers and return them to slavery, or ignore the clause in the treaty. The British found a way around this clause. They compromised by declaring that any American who came to New York and could prove beyond all doubt that he was the master of a slave, would be allowed to take him away. After that, those slaves who were not claimed would be evacuated with the army. Conditions at the time were chaotic and dangerous which made proof of ownership virtually impossible. Hence, few slaves with the British were claimed, and thousands taken away — 3,000, to be exact. Several of the vessels taking the loyalist contingents sailed north from New York to Nova Scotia, the nearest remaining British colony. The 3,000 Black Pioneers were dumped there in the frigid wastes. Their fate in Nova Scotia was, to them, as bad as slavery in the southern states. And to their epic of survival is another of the great stories of Black Survival in the face of impossible odds.

The story of those Blacks in the revolutionary affair has been one of betrayal by both sides — the Colonists and the Royalists. Blacks were used for convenience, but still they fought dreaming of that freedom, hoping for the liberty that was to be denied them. They are still fighting for it. It remains as far away as ever. But the real Dream must come true.

There was an airline advertisement couched in Bicentennial dress on one of the television channels going the rounds during the bicentennial celebrations of 1976: Robert Morley, a rotund, period piece of an Englishman, quite jolly and comforting, reassured Americans, in a voice so terribly English and juicy, that you could cut it with a stainless steel knife from Sheffield: "Do come visit us, Americans. We have forgiven you.

In all humanity, it would be too much to expect America's 22 or so million Blacks to find room in their hearts to echo Morley's sentiments.

REFERENCES:

Bennett, Jr., Lerone, *Before the Mayflower*
(Pelican Books, 1966)

Berlin, Ira, *Slaves Without Masters* (Pantheon Books, 1974)

Hodges, Norman E.W., *Black History* (Monarch Press 1971)

Miller, Major Donald L., *Black Americans in the Armed Forces*
(Franklin Watts 1971)

Rogers, J.A., *Africa's Gift to America* (Futuro Press, 1959)

Scobie, Edward, *Black Britannia*
(Johnson Publishing Company, 1972)

CHAPTER NINE

African Resistance to Slavery

"In slave resistance during the centuries of slavery in the Americas, we see that resistance, whether formal or informal, constituted a continuous battle of strategies between the slave holders and slaves."

–Vincent Bakpetu Thompson,
The Making of the African Diaspora
in the Americas, **pp. 1441-1900**
(Longman, 1987)

"Vengeance did not sleep. Historians who have made slavery idyllic and the slave an inferior people have little place in their work for accounts of this vengeance—this heroic anti-slavery struggle of the Africans."

–Herbert Aptheker

It is this epic of African resistance we must exhume from the buried pages of history and examine; for it is this continuous refusal to be shackled to the plantation that eventually broke the economic back of the slave system. This refusal to be enslaved was manifest in every area of this hemisphere, hundreds and hundreds of times, until the whole unholy business of enslavement of Africans crumbled into pieces. Plantation owners became absentee owners and scurried back to Europe to save their lives. It was this glaring fact that forced them to bow out with little grace and accept abolition and emancipation. By the time that happened, slavery had been reduced to ruins.

The idea that Africans waited patiently for their oppressors — who, in the first place, had put them there — to free them from their chains, is so much mythology. Resistance was mounted on plantation owners on a continuous basis, so that there was nothing else they could do but emancipate those that they had enslaved. By that time that monstrous system was destroyed beyond repair.

From the very beginning of the slave trade, resistance and rebellion were set in motion. When the Spanish ships with Governor Ovando sailed to Hispaniola in 1502 to reinvigorate the faltering colony that Columbus had left behind the previous year, a small group of Africans were being shipped to the island on that small voyage. Among them was an African Maroon, an anonymous slave who escaped to the Indians in the mountainous terrain of the interior soon after setting foot in the New World. Some 470 years later, there still lived an octogenarian in the forests of Cuba named Esteban Montejo, who had escaped from slavery in his youth and lived for years in those mountain hideaways. He must have been the last surviving example of this desperate yet frequent reaction to slavery in the Americas.

For nearly five centuries, the communities formed by these Africans dotted the fringes of plantation America, from Brazil to the southeastern United States, from Peru to the American southwest. These areas have been known at different times by different names like palenques, quilombos, mocamboes, cumbes, ladeiras, or mambises. They ranged from tiny bands that survived less than a year to powerful states numbering thousands of members and lasting for generations or even centuries. Today, their descendants still survive in semi-independent enclaves in numerous parts of the hemisphere. These descendants were found in Palmares, Cuba, Bahia, Jamaica and Haiti, to mention. Some remain fiercely proud of their African Maroon origins, and in some cases, faithful to unique cultural traditions that were forged during the earliest days of African history. The extent of violent resistance to enslavement has been well documented— from the revolts in the slave factories of West Africa and mutinies during the Middle Passage journey to the organized rebellions that began to overrun most colonies within the decade after the arrival of the first slave ships. The myth of the "docile slave" was exploded almost from the arrival of Africans to the plantations of the New World. Throughout the Americas and the Caribbean such African societies stood out as the heroic challenge to White authority; and, moreover, as the living proof of the existence of a slave consciousness that refused to be limited by the Whites' conception or manipulation of it. In other words, Africans did not accept that condition and fought it in any way and all ways possible, even to death.

Some of the penalties they had to face when attempting to fight their way to freedom were monstrous, indeed. The most brutal punishments had already been instituted for recaptured Africans, and in many cases these were quickly written into law. An observer in Surinam, on the South American Atlantic coastline, reported this bestial treatment of runaway Africans:

> If a slave runs away into the forest in order to avoid work for a few weeks, upon his being captured his Achilles tendon is removed for the first offense, while for a second offense his right leg is amputated in order to stop his running away; I myself was witness to slaves being punished this way.

But that was not all. Other inhuman punishments for marronage were castration and being slowly roasted to death while White crowds stood around enjoying their barbarity with devilish glee. That still did not stop the African warriors. Escape, at all costs, was an everyday part of plantation life in these Americas during the centuries of slavery.

An 18th century freedom fighter: Leonard Parkinson, was one of many Maroon guerrillas that were a permanent menace to Jamaica's white society.

AFRICAN WARRIOR

It was marronage and escape on a grand scale, with individual fugitives banding together to create independent communities of their own, that struck directly at the roots of this plantation system, presenting military and economic threats that often taxed the colonists to their limits. In a remarkable number of cases throughout, the Americas Whites were forced to humble themselves and beg their former slaves for peace. Treaties were signed with African Maroons in Jamaica, Brazil, Colombia, Cuba, Ecuador, Hispaniola, Mexico, Surinam, and Dominica. Haiti was a bird of a stronger Black color. The Africans did what all of the others should have done: not sign any treaty with their enemies. Instead L'Ouverture, Dessalines and Christophe, with thousands of African warriors, crushed the French to the ground and simply and literally took their freedom. It could have been done in all those other areas.

Initially, the signing of those treaties forced Whites to accept the Maroon communities, recognize their territorial integrity, and make provisions for meeting their economic needs. Unfortunately, in return for these conditions, White plantation owners sought an agreement to end all hostilities toward the plantations, to return all future runaways and, often, to aid Whites in hunting them down. Those treaties never should have been signed. Our African warriors should have realized that they were then in a position of great strength and should have acted accordingly. Up until now we, as Africans, face this same confusion. We cannot assess and do not know, or appreciate, our collective strengths.

African Maroon societies were not restricted to a few little isolated enclaves where runaways hid themselves as hunted creatures, venturing out only at the dead of midnight to seek food and drink. Far from that, they were in vast numbers everywhere in this hemisphere.

For instance, in Brazil, if Palmares was the most famous

AFRICAN MAROONS IN AMBUSH

and certainly the largest of all the quilombos, it was far from being the only one; the history of Brazil attests to the importance of collective flight and of resistance both to slavery and to the assimilation of White culture.

In his study, *Mixture or Massacre*, historian-activist Abdios Do Nascimiento attests to the fact that:

> These movements of armed revolt aiming at liberation and the fall of the slave system were found in all the territorial extension in which there existed a significant captive African population. They often quite took the form of quilombos like that of Palmares: organised communities of free Africans refusing to submit to slavery, and often were organised along the efficient agrarian economic and social forms of Africa.

In the quilombos of Brazil it was a war to the finish as epitomize by the 100-year war of the Palmares quilombo, led by the immortal leader, Zumbi. In the Recife revolt in 1824, also, it was an all-out war of liberty or death. The leader, Emiliano Mandacaru, issued a manifesto in verse to his warriors, which read:

> As I initiate Christophe
> The immortal Haitian
> Hey! Initiate his people
> O my sovereign people!

Abdios Do Nascimento commented that:

> In this verse is verified the inspiration Brazilian Blacks took from the victorious struggles of Toussaint L'Ouverture, Dessalines and Henri Christophe to liberate Haiti from the White domination of the French and to establish a sovereign state governed by Blacks.

There was no shortage of courageous African men of steel in Brazil, or in the other territories where the slave system operated. They led the struggle against their slave captors. While everyone remembers the lion-hearted Zumbi of the Palmares quilombo, there were also Preso Cosme and Manuel Balaio of the State of Maranhao who, in 1839, unleashed an intensive struggle involving 3,000 quilombo dwellers. In the state of Minas Gerais there occurred what has been described by historians as the phenomenon of an African who became a legend. Known as Isidoro the Martyr, he would lead his quilombo fighters of Garimpeiros into battle. Never once were his men vanquished in battle. In that category of superhuman quilombo leaders, the name of Manuel Congo comes immediately to mind. Crowned the king by his companions in struggle, he led his men in battle. This took place in the State of Rio de Janeiro when, in 1839, slaves rose up in arms, killing brutal foremen on a plantation called Fazenda Frequesia. They attacked other properties and then headed for the forest, where they sought sanctuary. Finally, one of the bravest leaders in the quilombo battles against the slave system was Louis Gama. Before a court of justice he unflinchingly made this final statement: "The slave that kills his master practices an act of legitimate self-defense."

The phenomenon of quilombos represents the resistance of a civilization that refused to die — a struggle in which African religion played a key role. All this African religious phenomena in the quilombos and other Maroon societies must be interpreted in the context of this climate of cultural resistance. For instance, when Boukman was opening the ceremony which was to herald the Haitian revolution, he and the African warriors called on Damballa: "We swear to destroy the Whites and all that they possess; let us die rather than fail to keep this vow." That vow was taken everywhere Africans were in revolt against slave tyrannies. In one of the mocamboes in Southern Bahia in 1692, the battle cry of the mocambo warriors was, "Death to the Whites and long live liberty." Generally speaking, the quilombo or mocambo or Palenque — whatever name we choose to call the African Maroon societies in the New World — tended to reproduce the African village. Once free from slavery, Africans rejected the elements of "western civilization" imposed by slaveholders and returned to their African roots, to the way of lie of their ancestors. Religious practices brought from Africa by the captured Africans were developed in the palenques. Africans living in their African communities made incessant raids on plantations, some even in broad daylight, and took their women and children away with them. In the palenques they organized themselves on the basis of the family unit. The palenque always maintained an active communication with the slave population in the mills, plantations and coffee and sugar fields. Communications were extremely important for the survival of the African warriors, and they worked in unison with and with support of the slaves on the plantations.

Africans who lived on the quilombos did not merely engage in a mindless escape to freedom, hiding from the cruelty and genocide of their oppressors. It went much deeper than that. In fact, a movement of resistance was formed in Africa in the fifteenth century, in the form of brotherhoods as early as the arrival of the Europeans. By the next century, this resistance had spread and the creation of quilombos in Brazil at that early date was linked to this same spiritual brotherhood started in Africa. It had passed on to the archipelagoes (Cabo Verde, Sao Tome) and reached the Americas with the arrival of captured Africans for slave labor. In his book *Mixture or Massacre*, the African-Brazilian (scholar-activist) Abdias Do Nascimento, makes mention that African slaves formed a secret society entitled *Ogboni*, which held a powerful influence in the struggle against slavery. A profound, multiform knowledge of this religious system is fundamental to understand the quilombo strategy that brought out in such communities as Angolares (Sao Tome), Palmares (Brazil) and others who fought using their African culture.

The religion or spiritual dimension is, of necessity, accompanied by a kinship – spatial, and moral; in other words, the African spiritual value system was the fabric on which the quilombo resistance was based. That spiritual belief went very deep and encompassed every aspect of life, both physical and metaphysical. This religious system, the Nyambe Brotherhood, covered the whole of sub-Saharan Africa with variants in the terms of description. The name "Nyambe" signified the sovereign, conveying order and reigning indisputably as the Father-Master-Lord who intervened against any power.

The African strategy of the quilombo was perfected in the Gulf of Biafra (Dikabo, Sao Tome); in Brazil (Palmares); in Mexico (Qujijila) in the sixteenth and seventeenth centuries; and in the Caribbean area. Professor A. Orlando Patterson of Harvard University stipulates that with the possible exception of Brazil, no other slave society in the New World experienced such continuous and intense revolts as Jamaica. This African resistance also reverberated in the Americas and crystallized near a few foci that intensified until they finally grew into open war against the colonial regime in the eighteenth century. In his study, American Slave Revolts, according to noted scholar Herbert Aptheker, over 250 slave revolts and conspiracies have been recorded in North America from the beginning of the founding thirteen colonies.

The main areas of intense warfare against the western value system of greed, barbarity, and genocide, using quilombo strategies, were in Jamaica against the English; in Dutch Guiana against the Dutch; in Guadeloupe and in Haiti against the French; in Cuba against the Spanish. Africans wanted no part of that inhuman system. The structure of the quilombo was complex and in terms of African society, had stability with military characteristics, but which was also a village or group of villages that could exist by themselves with chiefs and autonomous quarters.

The strategy used and the tactics, based on sudden withdrawals and attacks, confused the Portuguese slave traders. The quilombo defense was structured in a methodical way: every quarter could have been set on fire and left to stop the enemy's progress.

Quilombos were not occasional, scattered, and few settlements where slaves hid from their oppressors. They were found everywhere slavery existed. In Brazil, for instance, African resistance was organized as quilombos from the sixteenth to the nineteenth century, and carried on later to the entire period of the slavery system. In fact, quilombos were in existence everywhere against colonial society.

The European imagination, based on its materialistic value system, in which greed for the accumulation of wealth and power was the motivating force, could explain Africa, Africans, and their resistance to oppression only in European terms of bestiality and evil. Their narrowness, ignorance, brutality and false arrogance could never make them envisage African resistance within the framework of a specific religious, political, economic, social, cosmic pan-African Brotherhood System. It is around this base that is organized. The resistance in the Palmares quilombo, as in those elsewhere, will never be understood without a preliminary understanding of African civilization, and the high spirituality which controlled every move and mood of the cycle of life. This cycle did not die with physical death but continued in its metaphysical form with the African slaves. That was what they sought in their armed resistance against the oppressors. They were "reclaiming their minds." In the quilombos of Cuba, called palenques, Blacks rejected the narrowness and elements of western civilization thrust upon them by slaveholders once free from slavery and returned to their African roots, to the way of life of their ancestors.

The religious practices brought from Africa by the slaves to Cuba were developed in the palenques or quilombos. These quilombos were never destroyed but lasted until the War of Independence with Spain in 1868. African warriors from the quilombos played an important role in bringing victory to the nationalists. The Africans on the quilombos in Jamaica, Haiti, Dominica, and the Guianas were also unconquerable. Peace pacts and other practices of subterfuge had to be employed to prevent the total take-over of the Americas from the African warriors of the innumerable quilombos in the New World. In fact, in writing about the Saramaka Maroons on the quilombos in Surinam, a Dutch Governor of the colony likened them to the Hydra, the many-headed snake of Greek mythology that sprouted two heads for each one cut off. It is not surprising that the Saramakas for 100 years fought a war of liberation against the Dutch colonists.

In 1762, a full century before the general emancipation of slaves in Surinam, the Saramakas won their freedom. They were one of the six Maroon groups in Surinam who lived in quilombos and were never to experience long periods of enslavement. One other group of the six was the Djukas, who escaped from the slave ships and Dutch plantations in the late seventeenth and early eighteenth centuries and took refuge in the heavily-wooded and many-watered forests of the Guianas. The other four were: the Matawai, the Kwimti, the Aluku, and the Paramaka.

Strangely enough, one European historian came very near to giving an accurate definition of the quilombo. He, Richard Price, wrote:

> It seems safe to say that the phenomenon of
> quilombos represents the resistance of a civilization

176

that refused to die a struggle in which African religion played a key role , as much as a direct protest against the institution of slavery.

Put in blunt language, it simply means that Africans were determined at all costs to retain their African-ness. That is the legacy that they died to preserve.

In August 1800, one of the martyrs in the Gabriel Prosser Rebellion made this memorable statement of defiance. It symbolizes the indomitable spirit of resistance — even until death — which Africans carried with them throughout those centuries of slave oppression:

> I have nothing more to offer than what General Washington would have to offer, had he been taken by the British officers and put on trial by them. I have ventured my life in endeavoring to obtain the liberty of my countrymen, and am a willing sacrifice to their cause...I beg as a favor that I may be immediately led to execution. I know that you have predetermined to shed my blood. Why, then, all this mockery of a trial?

There was no shortage of African warriors who waged total warfare against the slave condition and were prepared to die under the most excruciating conditions for the total freedom of African peoples. The supreme case of this superhuman bravery occurred on occasions too numerous to tabulate. But one such case needs to be chronicled here. It took place in the ferocious Jamaican uprising in 1760, known as Tacky's Rebellion. Bryan Edwards, a historian, records that three African warriors were chosen "to make a few terrible examples of some of the most guilty." Edwards stated further:

> One was condemned to be burnt, and the other two to be hung up alive in irons, and left to perish

in that dreadful situation. The [one] that was
burnt was made to sit on the ground, and his body,
being chained to an iron stake, the fire was applied
to his feet. He uttered not a groan, and saw his
legs reduced to ashes with the utmost firmness and
composure; after which, one of his arms by some
means getting loose, he snatched a branch from
the fire that was consuming him, and flung it in
the face of the executioner...the other two never
uttered the least complaint.

REFERENCES:

Cameron, Gail; Crooke, Stan. Liverpool, *Capital of the Slave
Trade* (Liverpool: Picton Press, 1992)

Carruthers, Jacob H., *The Irritated Genie* (Kemetic Press, 1985)

Do Nascimento, Adbias, *Mixture or Massacre* (Buffalo, NY:
Afrodiaspora Puerto Rican Studies and Research Center,
State University of New York at Buffalo, 1979)

Montejo, Esteban., *The Autobiography of a Runaway Slave*,
edited by Miguel Barnet (New York: Meridian Books, 1969)

Price, Richard., *Maroon Societies*
(New York: Anchor Books, Doubleday, 1973)

Robinson, Carey., *The Fighting Maroons of Jamaica*
(Jamaica: Collins and Sangster Ltd., 1969)

Thompson, Vincent Bakpetu., *The Making of the African
Diaspora in the Americas 1441-1900*
(New York: Longman Inc., 1987)

Walvin, James., *Slaves and Slavery—the British Colonial
Experience* (Manchester, England and New York: Manchester
University Press, 1992)

CHAPTER TEN

The Haitian Revolution Explained

Whenever historians and others write or discuss the Haitian Revolution, the name of one man, and one man only, has always come to fore: the name of Toussaint L'Ouverture. While L'Ouverture was obviously one of the brilliant minds of the revolution, he was by no means the only one and not the only architect of its success. Had there not been the equally brilliant Jean Jacques Dessalines, who played a leading role in the revolution, the result might have been quite different. At the very beginning was the high priest Boukman, who really set the spirit of the Revolution. It was in the revolution planned by Boukman that Dessalines, a similar soul, joined and fought. There were countless others, too, who played pivotal roles in this "Liberty or Death" encounter, an encounter which lasted for thirteen years of massive bloodshed of African peoples, and even more of Europeans, who sought to enslave Africans and claim and control the land of Saint Dominique that was to become Haiti. The names of those others who fought gallantly for liberty are etched in blood in the history of the revolution. Best known among them are Boukman; Henri Christophe; Moise, L'Ouverture's nephew; Jeannot Bullet; Jean-Francois Papillon; Georges Biassou; Capois; Morpas; Clerveaux; Lamartiniere; Marie-Jeanne; Petion; and Magny.

Let us turn to the initial leader of the Revolution, the high priest Boukman. It was he who set the tone, mood, and spirit of what I must call the real revolution; that is, a revolution of enslaved Africans in Saint Dominique, which began on

GENERAL JEAN-JACQUES DESSALINES (1758-1806)

the night of August 22, 1791. Listen to Boukman's words of intonation at the Voudun ceremony as he prepares the stage for the struggle. He exhorts all assembled there with the words "Death to the Whites! Destroy Colonial Settlements! Black Domination!" He goes on:

> Good God who created the sun which shines on us from above, who rouses the sea and makes the thunder rumble; listen! God though hidden in a cloud watches over us. The god of the White man calls forth crime, but our God wills good works. Our God who is so good commands us to vengeance.

> He will direct our arms and help us. Throw away the likeness of the White man's god who so often brought us to tears and listen to the liberty, which speaks in all our hearts.

This evocation to Ogun, the God of War, was much more than a call to arms by Boukman. It was also more than a summation of the Black experience in Saint Dominique and indeed, in the rest of the Diaspora. Neither was the prayer merely an ideological statement. In fact, it was all of these, but of much more consequence; it was the expression of African consciousness.

The Haitian Revolution was not something that began with Boukman, Dessalines, L'Ouverture, Christophe, Jeannot, Jean-Francois and Biassou. It has been in operation in Saint Dominique, as in all areas in this hemisphere where slavery of Africans had been introduced. It was a continuous affair in Saint Dominique, as elsewhere. Since 1522, the Africans in that island, called Maroons, began their revolt against Columbus, followed by two others: one in 1537 and the other in 1548. These rebellions began as planters razing and abandoning the plantations and establishing free communities structured along the lines of traditional African societies. That was the

TOUSSAINT L'OUVERTURE

same pattern of resistance in Brazil, with the setting up of free African communities based on these same values. There was hardly a year that went by without an uprising and outright armed struggle between African leaders and their warriors against plantation owners and their paraphernalia of slavery with its ironware of violence and genocide. One of the most famous before the revolution in Saint Dominique was the Macandal rebellion, which started in 1751.

Francois Macandal was a Voudun priest and Muslim from Guinea via Jamaica, where he had been enslaved. In Saint Dominique where he was taken, he led a series of revolts that ended with the death of several thousand Whites. For his last campaign he planned to have Africans in the urban areas who were enslaved, and those on the plantations, to poison all Whites. A traitor among his people betrayed him and he was captured and executed. His plan, "Death to the Whites," became the rallying cry of Boukman and Dessalines during the 1791 Revolution. A soldier made the following observation of the revolutionary role of Africans who had liberated themselves and were living as Maroons in free African communities:

> It is from these brave inhabitants of the forests, these true founders of our liberty and independence that we should preserve forever as a preventative against surprise: that we ought to be perfectly on our guard before we suffer a crafty and perfidious foe to approach us; but; that the shortest and safest method is to keep as far as possible out of their reach, and never go near them without arms in our hands.

It is absolutely necessary to give this narrative picture of the conditions on his land leading up to the 1791 Revolution. For this revolution did not start cold out of the blue. It was born out of the non-stop uprisings which Whites had to face on the island when they tried to conquer and enslave Africans.

The rebellions and uprisings from the free African communities continued through such leaders as Santiago forcing the French and Spanish to offer a treaty to the Maroons in 1786. This treaty certainly did not put a stop to the revolts, because in 1787, uprisings were headed by Gillot and Hycinthe. Thus we can rightfully conclude that the African population largely wrote the history of that island right down to the events that are usually said to have triggered the revolution.

The picture that clearly emerges in looking at life in Saint Dominique prior to 1791 is that the guiding spirit of African life was one of rebellion and the quest for liberty. Death to the Whites and liberty were inextricably linked and intertwined. Africans did not conceive them separately or differently. Unfortunately, there were some who bargained for a guarantee of their own liberty in exchange for a truce with the Whites, leaving other Africans enslaved and the Whites alive. These arrangements were always broken by one side or the other. The lessons learned were hard but the Africans in Saint Dominique knew full well that it was going to be a fight to the death; in fact, total extinction of one race or the other. Boukman and Dessalines were very aware of that. L'Ouverture unfortunately did not share these thoughts especially in the later stages, when the Revolution was gaining momentum and the savagery of the Whites grew to unprecedented proportions. He paid the supreme price for discarding his Africanness and putting in its place the false image of France. France was his undoing.

History has called Dessalines all kinds of contemptuous names, such as an "illiterate" of which he was not ashamed. When spoken to in French, he would reply in Creole. Not so with L'Ouverture, who spoke French in a correct manner. Dessalines was labeled a savage, a monster, a fiend, a brutal murderer, a Black devil, and a debased creature. Frenchmen and women were mortally afraid o him. They cowered at the mere mention of his name. But they were jealous of the fact that he was a man who could inspire his men to near impossible deeds of the greatest valor. In fact, Rochambeau and Boudet of the Expeditionary Army, who replaced General Leclerc who had died, admitted in a letter written about Dessalines: "He is the only man who knows how to successfully wage war in the colony, we are only fifth-graders compared with him."

Added to that, he was even cleverer and more cunning that those untrustworthy, hypocritical Frenchmen like Leclerc, Rochambeau, Boudet and Etienne Polverel. That is why Rochambeau said to Boudet: "Under cover of the confidence accorded him, Dessalines conspires in silence." In other words, he outfoxed them at every move. The battle cry, which had been sounded first by Boukman, was to be taken up by Jean Jacques Dessalines. It was going to be a fight to the death. "Conquest or Death" was the battle cry.

Who was this man who was to play a victorious part in the revolution in Saint Dominique? Who was Jean Jacques Dessalines? Christophe, that other brilliant military leader, recalled the first time he had seen Dessalines: manacled, chained to a coffle, his dark body naked, head swollen from incessant beatings and streaked with red, a froth of blood on full lips, and his eyes in full blaze with frenzied anger.

Dessalines endured countless beatings. When they tried to convert him to the Christian faith by dragging him and several other Africans into a Jesuit church, he refused to budge, although in chains. He covered his groin with his hands where a whip's stock hit him a stunning blow. He heaved the contents of his retching stomach, and doubled over in pain. The brutish driver clubbed him unmercifully again and again and again. Dessalines fell on his knees, his lips a spongy pulp of red, one eye swollen shut and the other blinded by a rivulet of blood. These beatings were inflicted on him with regularity, for he refused to do the bidding of the man who had bought him. It was this savage treatment that stoked a blazing fire in Dessalines against all Whites. That fire was to burn relentlessly in all his military maneuvers against the enemy.

The mood of the 1791 rebellion was best exemplified by the words of first Dessalines and then Boukman:

> I, Dessalines, will disembowel every planter in Saint Dominique and drape their entrails on the Tchia-Tchia trees. I will gouge out their eyes and feed them to the fishes.

Boukman added:

> We cannot return to our native Guinea! The cursed Whites have brought so many of us here that we are like the seeds o the mocha plants. A thousand ships could not take all of us back to Senegal, Ghana, Zamesia, Somali, Katanga—to the hundred rivers and forests of our native land. And so we shall make this our Guinea!…We shall burn the canefields… smash the macerators…destroy the boiling sheds… and we shall kill all the Whites! Les grand blancs! Les petits blancs! Even the mustees and the mustifinos! We shall drive them into the sea! We shall run them into the hills and slaughter them! This land belongs to us. We shall kill les blancs! Kill them! Kill them! Who goes with me? Who goes with me?

Boukman's war plan was structured along five phases. One, the simultaneous self-emancipation of the Africans; two, kill all Whites and burn all crops in the area of cultivation; three, burn the cities; four, install camps populated by the men, women and children, and begin the cultivation of crops in the free African communities at the same time making raids against French reinforcements, and so decimating the European troops; and five, totally destroy the French forces, and then turn on the Spaniards and drive them from the eastern section of the island, thus dominating the island by Africans.

This was, in fact, a comprehensive battle plan in keeping with the goal of race vindication. The first month of the revolution was faithful to the revolutionary philosophy. The masses of Africans wreaked a path of destruction in the northern plains, setting buildings and crops aflame, and killing hundreds of White people. That course of activity resulted in moving the revolution as planned. But a surprising change came about when Boukman died, then Jeannot , who was assassinated by Jean Francois. The leaders (Dessalines excluded) began to petition the remaining Whites for peace. Perhaps this move was an act motivated by the leadership. Then came the great compromise by a document signed by Jean-Francois, Biassou and L'Ouverture.

These were the terms they requested:

General amnesty for all past offenses
Legal and complete freedom for a number of slave leaders—approximately 400
Abolition of corporal punishment
Three days each week for the slaves to work for themselves.

This great compromise was described as an act of treachery. It represented a different philosophy, motivated by an attitude that the alleged supremacy of the European way of life, including contempt for the Africans, was preferable. The new leaders, it felt, wanted to retire and live the good life as the Whites did.

At this point it was becoming apparent that L'Ouverture

was deviating from Boukman's philosophy. L'Ouverture justified these deals. He viewed the masses of his people as ignorant men who "did not know any condition of life more happy than slavery."

By August of 1793 L'Ouverture was showing change again; a change due to the influence of top leaders Dessalines and Moise. He agreed to revert to Boukman's plans.

Whites, with their reinforcements from France, were committing acts of the grossest savagery against Africans. It was then that L'Ouverture proclaimed to his people that he was going to fight an all-out war, and so move closer to the original spirit of Boukman and Dessalines. He promised:

Brothers and friends:

I am Toussaint L'Ouverture. My name is perhaps known to you. I have undertaken to avenge your wrongs. It is my desire that liberty and equality shall reign in Saint Dominique. I am striving to this end. Come and unite with us, brother, and combat with us for the same course.

Even so, L'Ouverture still tried to prove to the French that Blacks were indeed worthy of equality. That was what he wanted. His strategy was Black emancipation and White protection, something that was anathema to Dessaline. Even when he was elevated to Commander-in-Chief, L'Ouverture reaffirmed his loyalty to his previously stated commitment; so that "Whites, Reds, and Blacks" could now live in equality.

It was when, for a short period, L'Ouverture had absolute power as the Commander-in-Chief of Saint Dominique that he showed how westernized, or better, Gallicized, he had become. It was evident here that L'Ouverture had either not heard or had forgotten the words spoken by the President of the

Constituent Assembly in 1789 during the revolution in France. "We have not brought half a million slaves from the coasts of Africa to make them French citizens."

But L'Ouverture had another grave weakness which may well have accounted for his love-hate relationship with the French. For if we are to believe the statement by General Pamphile de la Croix, L'Ouverture had many love affairs with the White women of the upper class. One of them was none other than Napoleon's sister Pauline, wife of General Leclerc. In fact, the beautiful Pauline is suspected to have had many love affairs with other Blacks, among them, Henri Christophe. In his book *La Revolution de Saint Dominique*, General de la Croix states that when he opened one of L'Ouverture's trunks, after L'Ouverture had been taken prisoner by subterfuge, he discovered a secret compartment packed with love letters and other manifestations of love from society women to whom L'Ouverture had formerly been a slave. De la Croix went on to exclaim:

> Judge our astonishment when in forcing the double bottom of the safe that contained the secret documents of Toussaint L'Ouverture, to find tresses of hair of all colors, rings, hearts pierced with Cupid's arrows in gold, small keys, necessaries, souvenirs, and an infinite number of love letters which left no doubt of the success obtained by love by the old L'Ouverture.

The story ends that General de la Croix, realizing what terrible scandal the letters would have caused, destroyed them all. But let us return to L'Ouverture's political moves to create an integrated society in Saint Dominique. He (L'Ouverture) was finally free to start reconstituting the island by first setting up a constitution "of which justice and equality of right only, not of property, should be the basis." The men who advised him and framed his constitution "of which justice and equality

189

of right only, not of property, should be the basis." The men who advised him and framed his constitution were "for the most part White men; the most enlightened in the island." L'Ouverture filled "every public office with men of talents and letters in France." As was to be expected some of these advisors disagreed with L'Ouverture and did not support his ultimate policy. They wanted total authority and control. Eventually, other non-Blacks were appointed to replace them. They had the same intention.

It was blatantly obvious that such an arrangement in which Whites were allowed to frame a constitution of government for an island for which Africans had given their blood, was doomed to catastrophe. This constitution established L'Ouverture's versions of "liberty and equality" by abolishing slavery and declaring all people born in Saint Dominique to be French citizens. The composition of his government reflected this principle. While his army was controlled by his African generals and a few high ranking Mulattos, his civil administration was loaded with White and mulatto officials. And so one aspect of L'Ouverture's idea of equality was based upon merit rather than race. Naturally, the Frenchmen were ecstatic about his government since they held positions of control and power.

The foundation for L'Ouverture's colony was in his organization of the masses of Africans. The plan, in L'Ouverture's view, was set on a modification or reform of the chattel slave system. L'Ouverture decreed that the farm labor including "overseers, drivers and field-negroes who are subject to constant labor" were bound to "the plantations to which they belong," unless permitted to leave by the government. As you can see, not only did L'Ouverture continue the colonial economic order, he kept the old nomenclature "field negro" and even "field negress." This is unbelievable but true as the written records prove. L'Ouverture described this at the "new order" when it was so much like the ancient regime. The only differences were that the field laborers were paid one-quarter of the produce, the owners or managers one-quarter and the government one-half. Punishment of workers was removed from the hands of managers and owners and taken over by the government. Not only were the masses of ex-slaves returned to so-called socio-economic slavery under government control, but L'Ouverture also installed the White planters as proprietors or tenants to supervise the various levels of farm laborers. L'Ouverture went even further in imposing the slave machine once again on his people. All "overseers, drivers, and field negroes were bound to observe with exactness, submission and obedience, their duty." The government was the responsible authority for punishing offenders. Passes were required for any absences from work and owners were required to report the conduct of workers to the government.

This behavior of L'Ouverture must boggle the minds of all African peoples. There is no doubt that he was a great military commander but his African vision for his people was totally non-existent. It should not surprise us that European historians and others when they condescend to write about the Revolution place plaudits at the feet of L'Ouverture. He fought magnificently with magnificent African warriors and yet he was prepared to almost hand over the island on a platter to the French enemies.

Let us give praise where it is due and not view L'Ouverture as a traitor in the struggle for African Liberation. What was wrong was that he was too much of a trusting soul and his vision of liberation was living in peace with all races. It is inconceivable that an enslaved African should have been so trapped in the European ethic and believe that all would go smoothly with the government he wanted. The Frenchmen on the island were of other persuasions. Later events were to prove disastrous to L'Ouverture and his people. For the Europeans were to behave true to form. They wanted complete control of Saint Dominique, and to keep Africans in chattel slavery where they said they belonged.

L'Ouverture had strong beliefs about the running of Saint Dominique. He was of the firm opinion that agriculture and commerce were the foundations of prosperity; but prosperity for whom he did not stop to think. And, in truth he could not, because his advisors in the government that he himself had set up were predominately Whites and mulattoes. Yet he mistakenly believed that Saint Dominique under his brand of liberty, equality and civic virtue could be more prosperous than the old order of slavery. L'Ouverture must have known that those enemies whose lifestyle he admired would not tolerate any kind of equality with Africans whom they despised. It is to L'Ouverture's credit, however, that he demanded not only hard work but also accountability from White proprietors. No longer were they allowed to be arbitrary tyrants with the power of life and death over Africans.

Only the government could punish, ordered L'Ouverture. But who made up this government? The same tyrannical Whites.

L'Ouverture's whole intent was to set up a government based on strictly European lines. He wanted to make sure that all French citizens living on the island were safe and could go about their old business of exploitation. That was good for the Europeans but poison to the overwhelming numbers of Africans on the island of Saint Dominique. It was not going to work and it did not. The spirit voice of Boukman could not, would not be stilled. Most importantly, Dessalines was still there, and was going to change the course of events, and revert to the maxim — Conquest or Death. Death to the Whites.

In fact, Whites did not take long to show their true color.

L'Ouverture had not taken into consideration the fact that the Whites, whom he had protected under this banner, did not prove loyal when General Leclerc's expedition of 60,000 French troops arrived. In point of fact, they welcomed the expedition and clamored for the restoration of slavery. The vacillation of L'Ouverture in declaring Saint Dominique completely independent dismayed his followers, especially Dessalines and too, Henri Christophe. However, they remained within the army. The events which led to the arrival of a mammoth French battalion to take over the island convinced Dessalines that only the total expulsion of the French from the island would guarantee their absolute freedom.

In the meantime, a truce was arranged in which Leclerc and L'Ouverture in conclave were able to agree that the fighting was to be stopped and that L'Ouverture's generals were to be incorporated into Leclerc's army and that the liberty and equality of everyone were guaranteed. L'Ouverture was offered the post of Lieutenant Governor of the colony but declined and preferred to return to his home in Ennery as a private citizen, believing that his work was done and that the freedom of his people was assured. He was hopelessly wrong. He did not know those cunning Frenchmen with whom he had to deal. While it was obvious that L'Ouverture had judged those Frenchmen wrongly, yet he felt that Africans would rise again to a man, should the French institute subterfuge. What he was not aware of was the fact that they had fallen victim to that subterfuge. The French, using General Brunet, invited L'Ouverture to a conference. At this point he was warned most strongly by Jean Jacques Dessalines and Petion, the mulatto leader. Standing near Dessalines, Petion shook his head sorrowfully and said to Dessalines:

> But how could General L'Ouverture count upon sincerity of Whites, he their former slave, when I have not even the friendship of my own father for

the simple reason that I have African blood in my veins?

So L'Ouverture, unwise but trusting to the end, found himself ambushed and arrested, clapped in chains, and hurried on board a vessel, the Creole, which was moored in readiness for the capture. He was spirited away with his family to France. This incident occurred on June 7, 1802. It was an act of treachery of the worst order, something that Europeans used against Africans over and over and over again. L'Ouverture was to die in a jail fortress in France. As he embarked for France he warned the French:

> In overthrowing me, they have felled in Saint Dominique only the trunk of the tree of Negro liberty. It will shoot forth from the roots, because they are deep and numerous.

On this point L'Ouverture was absolutely right; it did not take long for those roots to start to shoot up. The removal of L'Ouverture did not mean the end of the Revolution. On the contrary, it gave the revolutionaries, particularly Dessalines and Christophe, greater force to fight and, if need be, to die for their liberty. In fact, the African Revolution was about to be fought by Dessalines. That brilliant leader said passionately,

> What have we in common with that bloody minded people?
> Their cruelties compared to our moderation, their color to ours—the extension of the seas which separate us—the avenging climate—all plainly tell us that they are not our brethren and that they will never become us.

It is important here to keep reminding ourselves of words of a poet wrote about Dessalines and L'Ouverture. These words we should repeat everyday when we wake up and have to face a hostile, racist society. Their meaning is still very relevant today. It is only when we accept them and act on them that we will be able to liberate our African minds and move forward to the year 2000. If we cannot do that then we are doomed to perpetual dependence as an African people. Dessalines is talking:

> Some things we do not need. Before we were carted to this land, cravats and powdered wigs we did not know. Some things L'Ouverture made sense only in some places. Food we will grow. Homes we will build. Our women and children we will protect with blood. With blood we made them free. We are all we need. We are all we have. We will sustain us.

But, let us go back for a moment and see what happened when L'Ouverture was treacherously removed from the island. Leclerc continued on his path of treachery trying to play one leader against the other; putting mulattoes against Blacks; and vice versa. He finally died of yellow fever. His successor, General Rochambeau, was the devil incarnate. He has gone down in history as the "Butcher of Haiti" and "Savage murderer of Haitians." He was thousands of times more brutal than Leclerc, and that is saying something. One historian recorded: "General Rochambeau maintained for awhile in Saint Dominique a regime at whose record of bloodshed and wanton massacre historians still shudder." But he reckoned without the leadership on the other side of Jean Jacques Dessalines who returned his savagery with equal ferocity.

For instance, one morning Rochambeau savagely tortured and murdered 500 African war prisoners in a frenzy of frustration after losing a battle. Dessalines countered by hanging 500 French officers right in the presence of the French army. When Rochambeau imported fierce man-eating hound dogs to hasten the genocide of African men, women and children, Dessalines made a vow that he would see to it

GENERAL ALEXANDRE PETION (1770-1818)

that the French eat every single one of those voracious animals. He set out to do just that by besieging the city where the dogs were caged. Soon the French began to run out of food, having been pinned on all sides by Dessaline's crack battalion. One by one they had to eat every single one of those dogs.

The final act of Rochambeau's humiliation came at the hands of Dessalines, a man he hated with a passion bordering on insanity. Rochambeau had proclaimed far and wide that when he caught Dessalines he would not hang him on a gibbet or shoot him as an officer would shoot another in battle. Rochambeau swore to his almighty that he personally would whip Dessalines to death as a common slave. But that was not to be. It was Rochambeau who was trembling like a coward when he and his soldiers were soundly beaten by the superior military power of General Dessalines and his powerful forces. Rochambeau pleaded, begged the English Navy to take him away from Haiti as a prisoner of war as quickly as possible, rather than leave him to face the fury of the victorious Dessalines.

When on that November 19, 1803, the French were almost totally wiped out by Dessalines and his warriors with Christophe, Clairveaux and Petion, Dessalines proclaimed:

> Let us swear to the whole world, to ourselves, to renounce France forever, and to die rather than to live under its dominion — to fight till the last breath for the independence of our country.

A few months before he made that statement, at a conference with his commanders of Arcahaye, Dessalines tore out the white from the French tricolor of red, blue and white and from that moment unfurled the symbol of Haitian Independence. He then intoned the chant, "Liberty or death," and had it inscribe on the new Haitian flag. The ancestral spirit of Boukman was still alive in Dessalines's words. When he issued his proclamation he stated:

197

The independence of Saint Dominique is proclaimed. Restored to our dignity we have asserted our rights. We swear never to yield them to any power on earth...Never again shall a colonist or a European set foot upon this territory with the title of master or proprietor. This resolution shall henceforward form the fundamental basis of our constitution.

Never before or since the Revolution has African independence been so clearly defined. Dessalines removed his colonial name of Saint Dominique and restored its former one before colonization — Haiti — which meant "high ground," "mountainous." Dessalines promised that Black the island was and Black it would remain. He said that the battles were over for now, but he advised eternal vigilance. He said that the revolution had gone into another phase and drafted a constitution, making certain that Africans would always have total control over Haiti. But after his assassination by divisive elements, both Black and mulatto, a new constitution was put into effect. Internal rivalries followed and Haiti became weakened and split by successive mulatto presidents whose loyalties had turned to France, the old enemy.

In ending, let us bring to mind again the warning of Dessalines:

You have done nothing if you do not give to the nations a terrible though just example of the vengeance that ought to be exercised by a people proud of its liberty and zealous of maintaining it... let us begin with the French. Let them shudder at approaching our shores, if not on account of the cruelties they have committed at least by the terrible resolution we are going to make—to devote to death whatever native of France should soil with his sacrilegious footsteps this territory of liberty.

Let us make certain, not only for Haiti, but for Africans everywhere that Jean Jacques Dessalines deeds of valor were not in vain. That is the clear lesson of the revolution in Haiti two hundred years ago. In fact, it was a lesson which spread fear in the hearts of the plantocracy from the southern plantations in North America to the entire Caribbean and the rest of the Americas.

Today, more than ever before, Haitians need the courage of Dessalines and those other heroic warriors who freed their country from French tyranny. The indigenous peoples in the hemisphere and indeed in the rest of this planet need to remember that lesson and act upon it in whatever ways necessary.

Napoleon furnishes an ironical postscript to the Haitian Revolution. A postscript that exposes the fact that he became wise after the dead. Maybe it is just as well that it is hindsight and that he did not put that plan into effect before the revolution. He seems to be placing the onus of blame for this major catastrophe on his Creole wife, Josephine of Martinique. In his *Memoirs of Napoleon* I he reflects sadly on this issue:

> The expedition to Santo Domingo was one of the greatest acts of folly that I have committed. I believe that Josephine, being a Creole, had a certain influence in the matter of this undertaking…a wife living in close companionship with her husband always exercises a certain influence on him.

> Colonel Vincent of the engineers was the only one whom I consulted concerning the proposed expedition, and he tried to dissuade me from the enterprises.

REFERENCES:

Rainsford, Marcus. *A Historical Account of the Black Empire of Haiti* (London, 1805)

James, CLR. *Black Jacobins* (New York, 1963)

Korngold, Ralph. *Citizen Toussaint* (New York, 1944)

Carruthers, Jacob H. *The Irritated Genie* (Chicago: Kemetic Institute, 1983)

Fatunde, Tunde. *Africans and the French Revolution,* African Commentary, Vol. 1, No. 2 (Amherst, MA: November 1989).

Fouchard, Jean. *Haitian Maroons,* translated by Dr. Faulkner Watts (New York: Edward Blyden Press, 1981)

De La Croix, P. *La Revolution de Saint Dominique* (Paris, 1820)

Levin, Benjamin H. *Black Triumvirate* (New Jersey: Citadel Press, 1972)

McTair, Roger. *Dessalines Talks to Toussaint L'Ouverture* (Savacou, Kingston and London: Caribbean Artists Movement, 1974)

Thompson, Vincent. *Bakpetu: The Making of the African Diaspora in the Americas 1441-1990* (London: Longman, 1987)

CHAPTER ELEVEN

Reparations

Time is running out for us
A deadline we must meet
To file Reparation petitions
And make politicians earn their seats
If we're to win this battle
Every organization must join the Fight
Then we'll tell our watchman
What's the hour of the night

–Queen Mother Audley Moore
July 27, 1950

Reparations for Africans are centuries overdue. It constitutes payment for 500 years of labor, of humiliation, of genocide on the slave hellholes of North, Central, South America and the Caribbean. It is also payment for the destruction and underdevelopment of the continent of Africa and the Africans there who managed to escape the European slave hunters roaming and burning the villages and towns of Africa, hunting for Africans to work their sugar-cane and cotton plantations. Africans also suffered the rape of their land and the colonial demoralization of their body and spirit.

For Africans, then, these quincentennial years should not be years of celebration of Columbus, the greatest enemy of the Indians of the Americas and the millions of Africans who were kidnapped and shipped as cargo to the Western hemisphere. There, under sub-human conditions of brutality, they were penned and chained to perform, as beasts of burden, superhuman labor for Europeans who had virtually wiped out the Indian populations from the tip of the Americas to the top. We must now organize an agenda for Black empowerment beginning with global moves for the repayment of reparations for centuries of suffering under the slave condition.

Hans Koning, author of the book *Columbus: His Enterprise,* illustrates the cruelty and infamy that Christopher Columbus practiced on the Indians of the Caribbean, which set in motion the later destruction of Africa and Africans:

> Columbus was cruel and greedy in small matters as in huge ones. He took the money reward for the first sighting of land, when the Pinta lookout actually deserved it; he wrote with glee of a fight he stated between the monkey with two paws chopped off and a wild pig. He had the Indian chiefs hanged and roasted on slow-burning fires to break all resistance against the forced collecting of gold dust in the streams. Indians who failed to bring in the gold quota he had set got their hands cut off. Men, women and children on Columbus's Hispaniola (now Haiti and the Dominican Republic) were hacked to pieces and the pieces sold from stalls to the Spanish solders for their dogs. It was considered good military policy to give those dogs the taste for Indians. The same natives who had welcomed the Spaniards as gods soon started mass suicide by eating poisoned roots and within two generations the Carib Indians were destroyed.

But, it was not "eating poisoned roots" that caused the almost complete annihilation of the Caribbean Indians. The Franciscan priest, Bartholomew de las Casas, tells this grim story in all its glory and macabre details: "The results of this license for ethnocide would never have been truthfully recorded with the thoroughness and detail that he brought to bear in his voluminous writings," so wrote author-historian Professor Jan Carew. Las Casas wrote:

> The Indians had a greater disposition towards civility than the European people, and that it was upon such people, the Spaniards, fell as tigers, wolves and lions all on lambs and kids. Forty years they ranged those lands, massacring Espanola, which in 1492 had a population estimated at three millions of people, scarcely three hundred Indians remained to be counted. The history of Espanola is the history of Cuba, San Juan, and Jamaica. Thirty islands in the neighborhood of San Juan were entirely depopulated. On one side of the continent, kingdom after kingdom was desolated, tribe after tribe exterminated. Twelve millions of Indians on those continental lands perished under the barbarous handling of the Spaniards. Their property was no more secure than their lives...As they rode along, their lances were passed into women and children and no greater pastime was practiced by them than wagering as to a cavalier's ability to completely cleave a man with one dexterous blow of his sword. A score would fall before one would drop in the divided parts essential to winning the wager. No card or dice afforded equal sport. Another knight from Spain must sever his victim's head from the shoulder at the first sweep of his sword. Fortunes were lost on the ability of a swordsman to run an Indian through the body at a designated spot.

The Spanish were so bestial in their behavior to the Indians that they did not exclude women and children from their satanic pastime. Las Casas exposed this inhumanity:

> Children were snatched from their mother's arms and dashed against the rocks as they passed. Other children they threw into the water that the mothers

might witness their drowning struggles. Babies were snatched from their mother's breasts and a brave Spaniard's strength was tested by his ability to tear an infant into two pieces by pulling apart its tiny legs. And the pieces were given to the hounds that, in their hunting, they might be more eager to catch their prey. The pedigree of a Spanish bloodhound had nothing prouder in its record than the credit of half a thousand dead or mangled Indians. Some natives they hung on gibbets, and it was their reverential custom to gather at a time sufficient victims to hang thirteen in a row, and thus piously to commemorate Christ and the twelve apostles. Moloch must have been in the skies...I have been an eyewitness of all these cruelties, and an infinite number of others which I pass over in silence.

These are a catalogue of genocide and a systematic destruction carried out on the Indians and Africans in this hemisphere from the time Christopher Columbus lost his way there. It is a catalogue of suffering 500 years long. These crimes have left a psychological scar on the native peoples of the Caribbean and the Americas. Justice through reparations must be done and must be seen to completion.

All these cold-blooded acts of murder were committed for greed of gold. Later on in this examination, a study of the exact tonnage of gold and silver stolen by the Spanish will be listed so that the claim for reparations be given stronger currency.

Added to those cruelties imposed on native Indians and Africans those others from Europe and Euro-America reaped billions and billions of dollars by African labor. With that money they developed and built their European lands. It was this African labor that put into motion a scientific and industrial revolution that produced untold riches for Britain, Europe, and North America.

Dr. Eric Williams, historian and former prime minister of Trinidad and Tobago, in his scholarly works, made this point clearly when he wrote:

> Tremendous wealth was produced from an unstable economy based on a single crop, which combined the vices of feudalism and capitalism with the virtues of neither. Liverpool in England, Nantes in France, Rhode Island in America, prospered in the slave trade. London and Bristol, Bordeaux and Marseilles, Cadiz and Seville, Lisbon and New England, all waxed fat on the profits of the trade in the tropical produce raised by the Negro slave. Capitalism in England, France, Holland and colonial America received a double stimulus—from the manufacture of goods needed to exchange for slaves, woolen and cotton goods, copper and brass vessels, and the firearms, handcuffs, chains and torture instruments indispensable on the slave ship and on the slave plantation. The tiniest British sugar island was considered more valuable that the thirteen mainland colonies combined. French Guadeloupe, with a population today of a mere 300,000, was once deemed more precious than Canada, and the Dutch cheerfully surrendered what is today New York State for a strip of the Guiana territory.

These Caribbean islands were at the time described as "glittering gems in every imperial diadem." Islands like Barbados, Jamaica, St. Dominique (Haiti), and Cuba were spoken of as magic names which spelt national prosperity and individual wealth. The wealth that these sugar barons garnered was proverbial. During those halcyon years when sugar was king, signs abounded in England and France stating that West Indian sugar magnates held the highest offices and built magnificent mansions and palatial homes. Numerous great houses were established in England by men who owed their opulence to plantations in the West Indies. Prominent among these magnates was William Beckford, son of Peter Beckford, the speaker of the House of Assembly in Jamaica in former times. Heiresses of these sugar potentates were sought in marriage by the scions of society. Sugar ruled the roost. It held the crown of position and wealth for those who owned plantations and slaves in the Caribbean. This caused Dr. Eric Williams to dryly observe: "Sugar was king; without his Negro slave, his kingdom would have been a desert." It was in that vein that Williams viewed the gross inequality which existed under this system of slavery where the plantation owners extracted untold riches while the enslaved African received no kind of pecuniary rewards for his time, life, and labor. Williams lamented, "This contribution of the Negro has failed to receive adequate recognition. It is more than necessary to remember it today."

Glorying in the financial boost which slavery gave to Britain, the late Sir Winston Churchill, former Prime Minister of Britain, and himself no lover of people of color, chronicled:

> Our possession of the West Indies gave us the strength, the support, but especially the capital, the wealth, at a time when no other European nation possessed the reserve, which enabled us to come through the great struggles of the Napoleonic Wars, the keen competition of commerce in the eighteenth and nineteenth centuries, and enabled us not only to acquire this appendage of possessions which we have, but also to lay the foundations of that commercial and financial leadership which when the world was young, when everything outside Europe was underdeveloped, enabled us to make our great position in the world.

If further proof is needed do hammer home the inestimable good that African slave labor did for the financial grandeur of Britain, the observation of the famous English actor and tragedian George Frederick Cooke should drive it home. One night at the Liverpool Theatre, Cooke staggered on the stage drunk, as was his custom. As soon as the audience noticed this, they began to hiss and boo him. A rising surge of anger brought Cooke to his senses and sobered him somewhat. Then he shouted back at them in his most professional and declamatory voice: "I have not come here to be insulted by a set of wretches, of which every brick in your infernal town is cemented with the blood of an African."

The history of Bristol, too, is written with the blood of Africa on its pages. Its buildings were built on capital accumulated from the sweat and labor of enslaved Africans. Its slave merchants became wealthy trading in the traffic of the slave trade. Bristol as a slaving port stood on equal ground with London until 1750. Nearly a thousand slave ships left the port every year to make the journey to the west coast of Africa and thence to the Caribbean.

It is necessary to know the magnitude of the profits and monies garnered from the slave trade and slavery, which literally financed the entire industrial growth and development of Europe, Britain, and Euro-America. On the other hand, when we look at the benefits gained by Africa and Africans on the mainland and in the Caribbean and Americas for the tremendous part they played in making Britain, Europe and Euro-America the highly industrialized, developed and rich countries that they are today, what do we see? A blank map – nothing but underdevelopment, poverty, and desolation. It is this gross, inhuman, inequality that we have set out to put right. The case for reparations is both urgent and valid. Until that cardinal sin is totally extracted, there will be no peace on this planet and no goodwill to all men and women who are the descendants of these plunderers. Until that happens Africans everywhere will remain second-class, inferior peoples at the whim and fancies and moods of the very Europeans who ancestors once kidnapped them and stole their land and labor, then left them to starve and scratch for crumbs as the pariahs of the world. That must not be allowed to continue to happen. It is for this important reason that we are calling for positive efforts for reparations once again.

Africa had been sucked dry of its numerous resources and its people. For Africans there was death and destruction everywhere. Today the world of Europe and North America and wherever else Europeans abound unashamedly are singing hosannas and paying homage to the architect of Indian and African genocide. No single Native American and African can involve themselves in these insane manifestations. They must show, like the great African American warrior Frederick Douglass did to a packed White hall in Rochester about the celebration of the fourth of July in the year 1852: "You can celebrate, I must mourn."

It was the late president of the Republic of Guinea, Ahmed Sekou Toure, who wrote a blistering indictment of the European-African contact and its devastating results for Africans. Sekou Toure accused Europeans of bringing contempt, desolation, exploitation, and despair. Their aggression was a total one: it was a cultural, spiritual, and military aggression, plus the destruction of nature, and even genocide. Sekou Toure claimed, and quite rightly, that "it was a time of indignity, want of responsibility, depersonalization and forced labour." Angrily and bitterly, he concluded in these words:

> It was a time of total disregard for the African since the personality, authenticity, dignity, and sovereignty which he had fully an completely enjoyed were being trampled under-foot. It was at this time that over 300 million boys and girls of our continent were exported to Europe, Oceania and especially the Americas—where they were used

as slaves, and where they tilled the land, built the cities, worked in the mines and accumulated wealth for the sole benefit of racist groups, which made their fortunes on the ruins and death of the people of Africa. It was a pathetic blood drain, which led someone to write that "the blood of the continent of Africa was being gradually drained into another in an endless flow." Never in the history of mankind had their been such horrors. A simple calculation of the number of people exported according to age, would reveal shocking results and would show how the 300 million figure is far below the actual figures, especially if we take into account the fact that for every slave who safely reached the coast, there were at least ten Africans murdered. Thus, those of our brothers today in the Americas are the descendants of the unfortunate slaves who survived.

Africans everywhere must mourn. But they have a more pressing important duty to undertake. They must, to quote Frederick Douglass again, "agitate, agitate, agitate."

In other words, they must take positive moves to turn this quincentennial and the immediate years after into a time of reckoning. A time for Africans to get their hard-earned rightful dues; for they have already paid for those dues with blood, sweat, five hundred years of toil, and death.

In other words, while the Euro-American world turned the quincentennial into a Hollywood carnival extravaganza in paying homage to Christopher Columbus for his navigational mistake in 1492 and the horrors it brought to Native Americans and Africans. Africans must have their carefully documented pay sheet ready to be presented to the nations who benefited from slave labor instituted by Columbus and imitated by other conquistadors. In other words, now is the time for Africans to put the final touches for reparations, something that started years and years ago. Make no mistake about it, the case for reparations is a very strong one indeed. In fact, there exists a historical precedent for the payment of reparations.

Africans everywhere must bring to fruition claims for reparations as soon as possible. If this is not put into motion quickly, then it will be a calamitous disaster for Africans on this planet. They can never get such an ideal time again. They will have to wait another 500 years; which means that they will have lost the chance of a lifetime, or better, five lifetimes. The time is now; it is the time to strike. Let us now, at this point, set about the examination of the case for reparations for Africans.

First of all, for other peoples, other races, reparations are nothing new. Monies and big monies have been paid to them for alleged ills they would have to suffer after they no longer enjoyed the free labor of enslaved Africans on their plantations. For example, some nations like France, Britain, Holland, Denmark, who owned slaves in the Caribbean, were compensated or their loss of slave labor when the system was abolished. It is important to elaborate on this last statement.

As far back as 1807 in Westminster, London, when a bill to abolish the slave trade had already been passed in the House of Lords, it was brought into the House of Commons by Earl Grey, then Lord Howick. The West Indian slave owners came forward then in order to claim compensation. They argued that utter ruin would fall on all their interests, and they would suffer the total loss of their income and property. This, they maintained, would be the inevitable consequences of the measure for the emancipation of their slaves. They prophesied that not only would there be insurrection and massacre throughout the whole of the slave colonies but indemnity would be required to the extent of at least one hundred million pounds sterling.

The planters and slave owners requested to be heard at the bar of the House of Commons, as they had been at the House of Lords, in support of their extravagant claims. Their request was granted and their cause was ably pleaded by Mr. Dallas, the late Chief Justice; Mr. Baron, the late Chief Baron of the Exchequer; and Mr. Scarlett, the late Attorney General who, in 1833, became Sir James Scarlett. In this debate, Viscount Howick, representing the government ministers, presented this issue with judicious care. He began by stating that he did not deny that:

> The apprehended loss which this measure might eventually cause, might become a fair question of future consideration. Let those who may conceive themselves entitled to demand compensation submit their case to the House, and if that case should be established, the House would never be backward in listening to the claims of justice.

Viscount Howick expressed this as a general principle. The West Indian slave owners, however, were not satisfied with this assurance, and one of their spokesmen in the house, a Mr. Manning, gave notice that he would proceed to move to form a committee to consider that the compensation should be granted, in the event of the Bill passing, to those whose interests would be affected by it. He then requested to know from Lord Howick, whether his Majesty's Ministers were authorized to assent to such a proceeding. Lord Howick's reply was that:

> It was contrary to the practice of Parliament to declare, beforehand, what might be the amount of compensation to be granted for possible losses by any general measures of political regulation or national policy which Parliament might adopt, and that therefore he was not authorized to consent to such a committee.

In 1807, the bill abolishing the slave trade was passed in the House of Commons without any expression being made, beyond this verbal assurance, for compensating what Parliament called "the eventual sufferers," or, to be more explicit, the West Indian plantation and slave owners. No such guarantee was even entered into or considered in the deliberations o the British Government of the question of compensation for the real sufferers — the slaves.

Parliament left its doors open to representations for compensation for the slave owners. In fact, it was a fait accompli that compensation would be paid. What had not been debated or agreed upon was the manner in which this vast sum was going to be paid.

So the matter was allowed to remain in abeyance for another twenty-four years, to 1833, before the issue was once more raised about compensation. The reason for this lapse of time is easy to explain. For one, slavery in those British colonies had not yet been abolished; thus, the free chattel labor of the slaves had not been affected by any legislation demanding their freedom. Slaves were still viewed in the eyes of the law as property of those who owned them. But now that the Bill for emancipation was being debated in the Houses of Parliament this was a bird of a different color. The climate for emancipation was now very favorable and slave-owners could see the loss of labor was about to become a reality. Hence moves for this compensation were being voiced and, in fact, made. While the general mood in Britain was in favor of some form of emancipation for the slaves, it was equally in accord with compensation for the owners of slaves. One of the prominent papers of the time, the Anti-Slavery Reporter, voiced this general attitude:

> We do not deny the right of the planters to prefer and to establish their claim to be compensated for any injury they may sustain from the great measure of national justice and policy, of converting the slaves into free laborers.

And so, the second round for compensation was about to be debated in Parliament on the major issue of emancipation.

The battle for emancipation turned out to be an uphill one. While the English populace was clamoring for passage of this Bill, inside the House behind the closed doors of Parliament preferred to procrastinate and defer their judgment. Finally the Abolition Act of 1832 was defeated by 136 to 92. The members of the House were more concerned in trying to define what the proper compensation to the planters should be; in spite of the fact that they were heavily criticized for being more concerned about compensation for planters than freedom for the enslaved Africans. One anonymous author wrote in a pamphlet entitled *Letters of the More Influential Classes* that "to the slave holder nothing is due, to the slave everything." The year after, 1833, not one word of mention was uttered in the speech from the Throne at the opening of Parliament concerning the abolition of slavery. Lord Stanley, the new Colonial Secretary and future Prime Minister of England, declared himself to be totally unsympathetic toward the previous proposals for emancipation.

Public opinion in London was rising in favor of emancipation. It could not be ignored. Petitions in abundance flooded the Houses of Parliament with over a million and a half signatures, the largest single petition being signed by 187,000 women, all members of the Ladies' Anti-Slavery Society. Add to that, a veritable procession of clergymen from the Established Church and the Dissenting Ministries marched on Downing Street, the home of the Prime Minister, to protest about the proposed compensation planned to alleviate the sufferings of the planters when the slaves (their property) were set free. This question was a point of heated argument with the growing anti-slavery brigade. They argued that slavery was illegal, and that compensation signified the acceptance of a legal basis to slavery. The rank and file in London strongly objected to what they termed "such a ridiculous and expensive hand-out."

Matters reached a head by May 1833. The government could not resist the mountainous surge of public opinion on emancipation any longer; so Lord Stanley outlined his guiding principles to the House of Commons. Further efforts to bring in amelioration were rejected and the system of compensatory apprenticeship was constituted to see that the planters would not suffer any "hardship through loss of labor." In fact, this scheme was only another aspect of slavery because it decreed that: "all slaves over six years old should continue working three-quarters of their time for their existing masters for a period of six years." But that was not all.

The most important clause of this decree was that government would "further compensate for the loss of a quarter of the slaves' labor, and the planters were to be loaned 15 million pounds (sterling)." To compound this gross injustice Lord Stanley stated: "It is quite clear that the repayment must be borne either by the produce of the Negro, or by the revenue of this country. It cannot in justice be borne by the planter."

What Lord Stanley was, in fact, saying was that the slaves would have to "buy" their freedom, as if by their unpaid slave labor, they had not already earned it many times over. Enslaved Africans were not "mindless property" cutting sugar cane with the fear of the whip always hanging over their backs. They were very human; skilled artisans who performed tasks that called for a high degree of intelligence and expertise. They performed such work as craftsmen, boilers, distillers, carters, tradesmen, coopers, and every other skilled trade needed in the production of sugar. As Dr. Eric Williams so correctly and bluntly observed, "no Negro, no sugar." The same observation can be made about cotton from the Southland of America. It is this inhuman and gigantic labor of Africans that demands, and in the loudest and clearest voice, reparations; and reparations right at this very opportune moment. However, it is important to go back and discuss those final moments of the slave institution in the British Islands of the Caribbean in 1833 when compensation for the slave owners was about to be given legal sanction by the British government. For the growing anti-slavery groups, Thomas Fowell Buxton, had long ago taken over as spokesman in Parliament for the sick and dying William Wilberforce.

It was the month of July. William Wilberforce, the English abolitionist had fought with yeoman courage as a member of Parliament in presenting this bill year after year before the members in the House. He was, by then, tired and spent. The measure was being debated by his successor, Thomas Fowell Buxton, while Wilberforce lay dying. The motion for this emancipation bill was tabled:

> An Act for the Abolition of slavery throughout the British Colonies; for promoting the Industry of the manumitted slaves; and for compensating the Persons hitherto entitled to the services of such slaves.

Parliament, as was to be expected, was insensitive to the injustices which were tabled in the proposals. The resolutions were carried by a comfortable majority. The bill in its fullest detail took two and a half days to be drafted by James Stephen. However, the abolitionists won because the apprenticeship period was amended to six years instead of twelve. What was more tragic was that they suffered a major defeat when the loan of 15 million pounds (sterling) for compensation to the planters was changed by the pro-slavery members of the House to a gift of 20 million pounds (sterling). The reasons given for this "gift" to the slave owners was not only specious but dishonest, arrogant and racist, as well.

Buxton made a spirited attempt to press for immediate and unconditional emancipation, but this only served to bring back the old hackneyed debate about whether or not Blacks were fit for freedom. This was argued most forcibly by Robert Peel who "was worried by the problem of amalgamating Black and White, and concerned about the Negroes aversion to hard labor." Other supporters of Peel and the pro-slavery faction contended that "the Negro slaves would be less fit for liberty at the end of the apprenticeship period than they were before it, because they would slip back into their slothful and idle ways without the whip on their backs." Anti-slavery voices refuted all these baseless charges with the statement from Daniel O'Connell that "Men who can bear slavery most assuredly offer a very strong presumption that they can bear freedom." That did not remove the grave doubts which members of Parliament held: that there would possibly be repercussions of even this controlled emancipation. They expressed great fears that when the Bill was passed in the House and it became law "there would be a subsequent bloodbath in the Caribbean Colonies."

The Bill for the Abolition of Slavery was, at last, introduced in the House of Commons on July 5, 1833. News was brought to the dying Wilberforce about the great debate which ensued. Sadly, he did not live to see this bill, which he had fought for in Parliament, enacted. As fate would have it he died two days before that historic day. The bill was passed on July 31, 1833, and became law on August 29 of that same year. Opponents of the bill waited in vain for this massacre. Once again they were shown to be hopelessly wrong in their assessment of the situation, for the freed Africans on the plantations wearily danced and rejoiced. No blood was shed, no one was killed.

The next day the emancipated Africans returned to work on the plantations at terms of the Emancipation Act. And what were these terms?

The bill, couched in conflicting language, contained two significant features: a transitional period of apprenticeship, and monetary compensation for the planters. The slaves were declared to be legally free, but it stipulated that they were to continue their labor for their former masters without remuneration for 7 ½ hours a day, six days a week, for six years. It was agreed that throughout this time (designated apprenticeship), these "apprentices" would receive their customary allowances. They would also be encouraged to work for wages at least 2 ½ hours per day so that they could accumulate enough monies to purchase their freedom before the apprenticeship time of six years had expired. Added to these unfair conditions of pseudo-freedom, their masters were to receive 20 million pounds (Sterling) as compensation for their losses of slave property. Edward Stanley made a very one-sided and dishonest statement in defending the principle of compensation when he said that emancipation could be achieved in no other way except by offering monies to the plantation owners for their loss of labor, and that this decision was consistent with honesty and justice. That the enslaved Africans did not receive any monetary compensation was of no consequence to British Parliamentarians or the public. Wilberforce himself, on his deathbed, made a remark about this situation, which does not do credit to the claim that he was a great fighter in the anti-slavery struggle. There are those who feel that it diminished a little of his glory when he observed: "Thank God that I should have lived to witness a day in which England is willing to give twenty-millions sterling for the abolition of slavery." That not one penny of this vast sum was shared among the slaves did not seem to have caused any quirk of conscience with anyone, not even to the dying Wilberforce.

One powerful voice was heard when compensation was being discussed in each European country involved in the trade. That voice was Victor Schoelcher's (the French's anti-slavery campaigner), who was in favor of compensation to the slaves. He expressed the view that "If France owes compensation for this social state which it has tolerated and is now suppressing, it owes it rather to those who have suffered from that state rather than to those who have profited thereby." His only concern, and it was a humanitarian one, was to compensate the victims of slavery.

Joaquin Maria Sanroma in Puerto Rico was another passionate anti-slavery fighter. Part of his address to the Cortes on February 17, 1873, illustrates quite clearly how Sanroma felt about this question of compensation: "Do you wish a grand measure or the preparation of the slave for freedom? Give him the compensation money which we reserve for his owner." Needless to say, Schoelcher and Sanroma were overruled. The metropolitan governments saw fit to give compensation only to the plantation owners who were the beneficiaries of slavery. This caused Dr. Williams to observe:

> It was the compensation not for the deprivation of liberty but for the expropriation of property. Much has been written about the magnanimity to the planter and not the slave. No requirement was imposed that the money should be used to finance the necessary rationalization of the Caribbean sugar economy. The planter was free to dispose of his money as he pleased; the absentee interests for the most part withdrew from the West Indies altogether.

It was not only the British who got compensated for their slaves. Compensation in the French colonies totaled 150 million francs. Denmark paid their slave owners in the Danish Virgin Islands 5,500,000 francs — about two million dollars. The Dutch government settled for compensation of over 16 million florins, to which the emancipated slaves themselves had to contribute some of this money. No compensation was given in Cuba since the Spanish government could hardly insist that the planters who had joined in the revolution receive compensation that they themselves had rejected. The situation in Haiti posed some problems. President Boyer came to an agreement in 1825 to pay over to the French a demand for an indemnity of 150 million francs in six annual installments. This imposed the added financial burden on the infant independent state of Haiti, which severely crippled its development in those early years.

The British paid the largest compensation to the English slaveholders on their colonies in the Caribbean since Britain had the highest number of slaves in those islands. To better understand this situation it is well to examine how the British went about the settlement of compensation. What conditions did they employ to calculate what they ironically termed a just payment?

Each island worked out the compensation that should be given to individual planters. This was calculated from the ratio of the quantity of exports to the number of slaves. In that manner the assessment of the slaves' productivity could be ascertained in each island. Consequently, in the colonies where there were few slaves, the ratio was high and the compensation was correspondingly high. For example, in Trinidad and British Guiana, where there were small numbers of slaves, output was relatively high; so that compensation for a headman in British Guiana could reach as high as 230 pounds. The following figures give an estimate of the average compensation per slave paid to plantation owners on some of the islands: British Guiana, 58.10 Sterling; Trinidad, 56; Jamaica, 20; Barbados, 21; St. Kitts, 17; Antigua, 15; Bermuda, 12. Compensation was paid for a total of 668,000 slaves who were, at the time, on plantations on all of the English-speaking Caribbean islands: Antigua, Barbados, British Guiana, Dominica, Grenada, Jamaica, Montserrat, Nevis, St. Kitts, St. Lucia, St. Vincent, Tobago, Trinidad, and Virgin Islands. Other contemporaries give the figure of slaves during that time at 800,000 in 19 British colonies. Naturally the price per slave fluctuated. Older men and women, and young children over the age of six years, were priced much lower than the men. Children under the age of six were not priced.

The payment of compensation to British and European slave owners has had a deep and lasting effect on the development of their countries. For them, it was a positive one, which placed them in advance of Africa and African peoples. To repeat that the seeds of world capitalism were sown on the sugar plantations and on the backs of Africans who toiled and labored without a penny of compensation until death in the Caribbean and in the Americas is one of the understatements of this dying twentieth century. It was, above everything else, a psychological disaster, from which African peoples have not yet recovered in these last 500 years. To heal this psychic wound, and put Africans on par with countries that robbed them for centuries, reparations must be paid, as it has been paid to the peoples who have suffered miniscule holocausts nowhere comparable to the horrors Africans endured from the slave masters of Europe, Britain, and North America.

It was not only morally dishonest to pay these vast sums of compensation to slave plantation owners who behaved with criminal indifference to millions of Africans over an inordinately long passage of time, it was greed of the lowest order. But the criminality of this behavior was that it gave the world of Europeans absolute power over the world of Africans in all things.

What this absolute power meant to Europeans, right from the beginning, was that Africans were imprisoned not only in body but in mind, as well, while their lands were sucked dry and they had to labor under penal conditions for the industrial development of their captors. That this state endured for centuries has had a devastating effect on the bodies, lands, and of even more importance, the minds of Africans. To seek reparations for this massive destruction of a people is not requesting too much. In fact, it is too little, especially when one realizes that other peoples who suffered less infamy received very adequate compensation for their agonies.

Japanese-Americans, for instance, were paid reparations by the United States government for a five-year internment during World War II, which was as it should have been. The government has not even apologized for nearly 500 years of African slavery and centuries of overt persecution. It is clear to see that "race" is a determining factor in this affair.

Tony Brown, the producer-director of Tony Brown's Journal on TV Channel 13, made this point quite clearly when he said:

> Africans were enslaved because of their race; and built America's infrastructure and economy for the same reason. The slave trade, for example, built Brown University. Is that fair? That use of race as a "determining factor" is precisely at the core of today's disadvantage as the Supreme Court has been trying to tell us for the last 30 years. Racism bred poverty and poverty bred disadvantage and this lack of opportunity fuels the need to consider race…

And all this can be traced right back and directly to the callous manner in which Africans were thrown after centuries of imposed underpaid hard labor, while the enslavers were given the golden handshake, shown great generosity and unbelievable humanity. This condition must not be allowed to continue into the next century. If it so happens then Africans will remain the pariahs of the world, begging to consume the scraps that remain on European plates. A political, constitutional, legal, economic fight must be mounted at the highest level, and pursued by Africans and African organizations everywhere on this planet. That must be part of the African agenda for the coming years while Europe still honors the man who once set this disaster into motion.

One can make the case for reparations even stronger. It was not only British and European slave owners, and the Japanese-Americans, who received compensation. American slave-holders, not only in the Southern states, but Northerners, who gave the commercial impetus with their slave industries and manufactured commodities needed by the slave system, they, too, became the wealthy power-brokers of America. It is little wonder that vast areas of land-property are still in the hands of the descendants of these pernicious slaveholders. One is reminded here of something that Professor Kenneth Stampp in his study on slavery titled, *The Peculiar Institution,* stated: that it was not "the Negro" who should be ashamed of slavery but the South, and White Southerners who waxed grotesque on cotton and on the pickers of cotton, Africans. Cotton was so fundamental to the economic growth of America that up to the eve (1860) of the Civil War, the cotton industry produced 57% of the wealth of America. One does not have to strain his or her mental powers to know who were the main and only beneficiaries of this 57% wealth. Africans in this land did not even receive the mule and the so-called forty acres promised them. Payment is long-long-century years overdue. And we are not here referring to a mule and some forty infertile acres in the mud and dirt of the South. What we are talking about is billions and billions of monetary compensation.

Let us be brutally frank. It is not only the 60,000 Japanese-Americans who survived the detention camps in the northwest region of the United States during World War II who deserved, and deservedly so, compensation; compensation that amounted to approximately $20,000 per person, or a total of $1.2 billion. Other figures given are $1.5 billion. It does not really matter which of these two totals is correct. The point of the matter is that very substantial reparations were paid to the Japanese-Americans for the inhumanity meted out to them by the United States Government during World War II. And rightly so!

Nazi Germany, which took its ideology of White supremacy to its ultimate in the savage extermination of 8 million Jewish people in the gas chambers of their concentration camps during the Second World War, made positive overtures to pay Jewish survivors of these death camps substantial reparations. In the early years of the sixties there was much debate in Israel whether this money should be accepted. However, the fact of the matter was that this offer was made, and in very many cases it was accepted. To date, it has been stated that the German government has paid over $80 billion for these horrendous atrocities against the Jews.

Going further back into the centuries, in the very same year (1492) that Columbus made his navigational sortie of error, hundreds and thousands of Sephardic Jews and African and Arab (mixed) Moors were murdered and/or expelled from Spain. Today, 500 years later, Spain is honoring Sephardic Jews. But not the African-Arab Moors! This statement about honoring the Sephardic Jews appeared in *the New York Times International*, Sunday, June 3, 1990. It read:

> The Prince of Asturias Foundation, a private organization linked to the Spanish royal family, announced in the northern city of Oviedo that it was granting its annual Concord Prize to 700,000 Sephardic Jews around the world. The 21-member jury, which includes some of Spain's most powerful business leaders, said in a statement that after five centuries of estrangement, the prize was being given "to reach out to those communities, opening forever the doors of their original country." The Asturias award will be

given in Oviedo in October by Prince Felipe.

The contributions of the Moors in Spain and Portugal from 711 to 1492 AD lie forgotten in the hidden pages of history. The Afro-Iberian Moors were responsible for almost all the geographical lore which the Europeans, primarily the Portuguese and Spanish, used in their global expansion. Their intellectual, navigational and scientific brilliance have been written out of history. They, like the millions of Africans on this planet, remain in a twilight world, still at the mercy of those who oppressed, exploited, butchered, maimed, and murdered them and stole their resources and lands. Those guilty nations must and, I repeat, must be made to pay Africans for this gross inhumanity.

Even Pope John Paul II had to beg forgiveness for Christians involved in the slave trade. He did that in February 1992 when he journeyed along the same route the millions of Africans passed on their terrible route across the Middle Passage to the world of the Americas and the Caribbean. Standing at the "door of no return" on the slave fort-prison of Goree Island near Dakar in West Africa, Pope John Paul II said: "How can one forget the enormous suffering inflicted, ignoring the most elementary rights of man, on the people deported from the African continent...From this African sanctuary of Black pain, we begged the pardon from above." He likened the prison where Africans were penned awaiting the slave ships, to this century's concentration camps in Germany. The *Maison des Esclaves*, as the fort has been named, has been restored and renovated as a museum to document this savagery and horror; savagery which caused two African-American top entertainment stars, Dionne Warwick and Isaac Hayes, to weep unashamedly when they visited these slave dungeons. Many African women who have entered these dungeons in which their ancestors were held have been heard to shriek with horror and recoil with fear and trembled on their visits to these prisons. The film

"Sankofa" brings to life most poignantly the horrors Africans suffered in these European-built holes of hell.

Not satisfied with what he had seen on Goree Island, the Pope still went about the quincentennial year with an air of penitence. In October 1992 during a visit to Santo Domingo in the Dominican Republic that Columbus named Hispaniola, the Pope pleaded with Native Americans to forgive the White man for 500 years of injustices and offenses. He pleaded: "In the name of Jesus Christ and as Pastor of the Church, I ask you to forgive those who have offended you. Forgive all those who, during those 500 years, have been the cause of pain and suffering for your ancestors and yourselves."

While it is noble to forgive, Africans want more than forgiveness from Europeans and Anglo-Americans who enslaved, tortured and murdered them. Everyone of those European nations, not forgetting Anglo-Americans, engaged in the slave trade and slavery benefited in terms of money from that evil trade and institution. It is a fact known by every schoolboy and schoolgirl who has been taught the truth about slavery that the industrial revolution was financed by the massive profits from sugar and cotton and other materials necessary to the trade. In his classic work *Capitalism and Slavery*, Dr. Eric Williams details the investments of profits made from the triangular trade. High up on Dr. Williams' list is banking. There was scarcely a Merchant Bank in London, Liverpool, Glasgow, or Bristol that did not owe its beginnings to monies garnered from the slave trade and slavery. No less than the world famous insurance body of Lloyds of London had similar beginnings.

Williams records that:

Many of the eighteenth century banks established in Liverpool and Manchester, the slaving metropolis and the cotton capital respectively, were directly associated with the Triangular Trade. Here large sums were needed for the cotton factories and for the canals, which improved the means of communication between the two towns.

Among some of the men in Liverpool who achieved fame and fortune from the slave industry and whose prestige, wealth and power are being still enjoyed by their descendents from Liverpool were Robert Cunliffe, Thomas Leyland, Richard Gildart, and Arthur Heywood.

Cunliffe, with his father, Foster Cunliffe and his brother Ellis, owned four slave ships which together could hold 1,120 slaves. Ellis was a Liverpool Member of Parliament for twelve years.

Thomas Leyland, one of the richest men in Liverpool, was Mayor of the seaport town for three terms. Between the years 1782 and 1807, he transported over 3,000 slaves to Jamaica alone. In 1807 he established his own bank, Leyland and Bullin, which eventually became part of what is now the Midland Bank, one of Britain's top banks.

Gildart was the brother-in-law of Robert Cunliffe. He was three times Mayor of Liverpool and a Member of Parliament from 1734-1754. With his sons he owned three slaving vessels.

Heywood and his brother made fortunes in the slave trade and became bankers. Their firm merged with the Bank of Liverpool, later known as Martin's Bank, which in turn was absorbed by Barclays Bank, a British bank with an international reputation.

As one can notice, close family ties in banking and industrial circles made these men powerful in international banking, business, trade, and commerce. Dr. Williams explained this habit of close family ties in business:

Typical of the partnership of inter-relationships of the time, the daughter of one of the partners of the Heywoods later married Robertson, son of John Gladstone, and their son, Robertson Gladstone, obtained a partnership in the bank in 1788. The firm set up a branch in Manchester at the suggestion of some of the town's leading merchants. The Manchester Branch, called the "Manchester Bank," was well known for many years. Eleven of fourteen Heywood descendants up to 1815 became merchants or bankers.

As noted earlier, the only peoples who received absolutely nothing for this massive extended plunder of their riches and land, and for their centuries of unpaid labor, were Africans. Even the gold and silver in the hemisphere of the Americas and the Caribbean were plundered and shipped to Europe, particularly Spain, to enrich the impoverished European nations. It has been estimated that between 1503 and 1660 (just over a century and a half), close to 200 tons of gold was stolen from the Americas and shipped to Spain. During that time, 17,000 tons of silver was spirited away as well. The value of all this has been put at 28 billion dollars.

After the Berlin Conference in 1887, the Motherland of Africa was carved up by European imperialists for themselves and their generations. They waxed fat and rich and gross on the blood, flesh, land and resources of Africa. They must be made to pay back big monies for this ruthless banditry.

In the United States, several organizations and Black leaders and congressmen (particularly Queen Mother Moore, Congressman John Conyers, and Senator Bill Owens) have been working steadily on the issue of reparations for several years. Organizations, too, like the National Coalition of Blacks for Reparations in America (N'COBRA) have been involved in the reparations struggle. Another standard bearer is the

Marcus Garvey movement, the Universal Negro Improvement Association, headed by its president, Marcus Garvey, Jr. The UNIA has held several seminars, conferences, and lectures on the issue of reparations.

Since the statement made by President Ibrahim Babangida of Nigeria, for the "World Conference on Reparations for Africa and Africans in the Diaspora," which was held in Lagos on December 14-15, 1990, the issue of reparations has been placed on the front burner by African world leaders. "Demanding reparations is not meant to build a world of racial exclusivity but a partnership built on mutual respect," stated President Babangida. At the 27th Ordinary Assembly of the Organization of African Unity (OAU) held in Abuja, Nigeria in June 1991, President Babangida, who is the OAU Chairman, made the position on reparations very clear when he said:

> On the issue of international indebtedness to and by Africa, the truth is that the legacy of the past weighs too heavily on the present and casts a shadow on our future capacity to develop our economies. There was the triple tragedy of slavery, colonialism, and neocolonialism. In the absence of a desirable comprehensive and substantial outright reduction in the debts magnitude, credit or countries must, at a minimum, support a complete suspension of the debt service for a very long period. Africa is neither asking for something new, nor extraordinary, or unjust. All we ask is to be treated as other peoples have been treated: that the admission of wrongdoing must be accompanied by restitution. We demand that it be recognized by all that reparations represent the missing link in our difficult quest for international justice, peace, and progress.

The question of reparations is the order of the day.

More and more worldwide organizations are joining together for a strong movement seeking reparations.

Dr. Yusuf N. Kly, professor in the School of Criminal Justice at the University of Regina in Canada, stated recently: "International law provides the moral and legal basis upon which a people can seek reparations."

However, all avenues are being examined. Africans are seeking heavy monetary compensation for enslavement, dehumanization, and preventing the race from progressing in society.

Reparations was defined by the Honorable Silis Muhammed, Chief Executive Officer of the Lost-Found Nation of Islam, in these words: "Reparations is the key to economic freedom—the end of 400 years of bondage for African-Americans; in fact, for Africans everywhere."

No stone is being left unturned in the quest for reparations; from the UN, Congress, African and Caribbean governments, the Senate, European governments to international courts of justice, all are being brought into this global struggle for justice and compensation. In fact, reparations has top priority in the Black agenda up to the year 2000. This was decided at the inaugural meeting of the Black Think Tank (BTT) of the Pan African Movement held on August 1-8, 1992, at Ascon, Topo, Badagry, Lagos, Nigeria. The Seventh Pan-African Congress ("For Control of the World") met in 1993.

The situation for Africans is critical. African-American scholar Dr. David H. Swinton in his statistical survey, "The Economic Status of Black Americans: 'Permanent' Poverty and Inequality," exposed the "disadvantaged economic status of the the African-American population" and concluded that it is a "permanent feature of the American economy." He concluded that, "the only viable option is a program of reparations. A constructive and well-designed program of reparations will bring an end once and for all to racial inequality." That applies not only to African-Americans but Africans anywhere on this planet. One of the most influential Nigerians, Chief Moshood Kashimawo Abiola, insists that the western countries owe Africa for slavery. He has one consuming passion: to have White people in Europe, the United States and the Middle East repay Africa and Africans everywhere for the damage done by the slave trade and slavery. Africans are of one accord on this issue of reparations.

Never in the annals of human history has there been a case more deserving of compensation than the forced enslavement of millions of Africans on the plantations of North America, the rest of the Americas, and the Caribbean, to perform manifold duties of labor without wages. The voice of humanity cries out for reparation s in order to set the record right. A persistent denial of this right to reparations can only mean a denial of the rights of Africans to a common humanity enjoyed by all other races that inhabit planet Earth. Africans must not accept this sub-human condition. They are duty-bound to set in motion a global revolution for reparations, by any and all means at their disposal.

END.

REFERENCES:

An Essay on the Abolition of Slavery, printed by W.P. Penny
(London, 1833)

Augier, F.R.; Gordon, S.C.; Hall, D.G.; Reckford, M. *The
Making of the West Indies*
(London: Longmans Green & Co., 1960)

Brady, Terence and Jones, Evan. *The Fight Against Slavery*
(New York: W.W. Norton & Co., Inc., 1977)

Carter, E.H.; Digby, G.W. *History of the West Indian Peoples*
(London: R.N. Murray Nelson, 1954)

Dookham, Isaac PhD. *A Pre-Emancipation History of the
West Indies.* (London: Collins, 1972)

Ethnocide of Indians by Spaniards (Diary of Los Casas) –
History of the Indies (1874-1566)

Green, William A. *British Slave Emancipation*, 1830-1865.
(London: Oxford University Press, 1976)

Jamaica: By a Retired Military Officer (London 1835)

Koning, Hans. *Columbus: His Enterprise*
(New York: Monthly Review Press, 1976).

Van Helmond, Marji; Palmer, Donna. *Staying Power—Black
Presence in Liverpool* (Liverpool 1991)

Nelson's West Indian History
(London: R.N. Murray Nelson, 1971)

Plimmer, Charlotte & Denis. *Slavery—The Anglo-American Involvement.* (United States: Harper and Row, Inc., 1973).

Robinson, Cedric J. *Capitalism, Slavery and Bourgeois Historiography* (unpublished)

Scobie, Edward. *"The Moors and Portugal's Global Expansion," Golden Age of the Moor,* edited by Ivan Van Sertima (New Brunswick, New Jersey: Transaction Publishers, 1991)

Sherlock, P.M. *West Indian Nations.* (London: Macmillan, 1973)

Williams, Eric. *Capitalism and Slavery.* A Perigree book (New York: GP Putnam and Sons, 1980)

—————*From Columbus to Castro: The History of the Caribbean.* (London: Andre Deustch, 1970)

B. Journals

Wilcox, Preston, *"Urban Marshall Plan, No; Reparations, Yes,"* Journal-Observer, March 29, 1990

"Africans in the Diaspora Deserve Dual Citizenship," Muslim Journal, January 11, 1991.

"Pope Begs Forgiveness for Christians in the Slave Trade," Rockland Journal-News, February 23, 1992.

C. Magazines and Newspapers

"Babangida's Bold New Initiatives," African Connection, October 1991.

"Apprenticeship and Emancipation," Caribbean Quarterly, volume 3, number 3. Department of Extra-Mural Studies, University of the West Indies, Mona, Jamaica. Reprinted with permission.

"Nigeria Puts Reparations on OAU Agenda," Daily Challenge, May 29, 1991

Pope John Paul II, *"Forgive the White Man for 500 Years of Injustices,"* Daily Challenge, October 14, 1992.

Williams, Denis A. *"Reparations: The Big Payback,"* Emerge Magazine, Volume 2, Issue 7, May 1991.

"How Much Gold and Silver Was Plundered in Our America," Gramma, May 6, 1990.

Pringle, Rachel. Islander, Vol. II, Number 3, St. Lucia.

"Nation of Islam Goes to United Nations," Muhammad Speaks, Volume 8, Number 6.

"A Niggardly Negro that President Bush Should Fire," Network News, comments by Tony Brown, January 1991.

"Worsening Black Economy Requires Reparations, Argues Black Economist," New York Amsterdam News, July 13, 1991.

"Spain Honoring Jews 500 Years After Expulsion," New York Times, June 3, 1990.

"An Influential Nigerian Insists West Owes Africa for Slavery," New York Times, August 10, 1993.

"Intensifying the Struggle for Human Rights," The Black Collegian, September-October 1990.

"Reparations: At Home and Abroad," The Final Call, July 27th, 1992.

APPENDIX

Repatriation

The inaugural meeting of the Black Think Tank (BTT) of the Pan-African Movement took place from 1-8 August, 1992, at Ascon, Topo, Badagry, Lagos, Nigeria. The BTT was attended by Black leaders and intellectuals representing all regions of the Black world. They examined the issues: "Why are we not benefiting as a people from the civilization we pioneered and what are we to do to get back on our feet again as one family?" The Black Agenda is the product of their deliberations and it lays down the rules to guide the activities of Black governments, individuals, organizations, communities, family units, institutions from now until the year 2000.

REPATRIATION AND DUAL CITIZENSHIP

1. Every Black person in the Diaspora has the right of repatriation, the right to return and settle in the homeland, in any African country of their choice. African governments are to reach out to them, set them up in programs to make their return as comfortable and fruitful as possible, and accord them full opportunity to fulfill their talents and expertise in service to the Motherland.

2. Every Black person in the Diaspora has the right of citizenship in an African country of his or her choice. US Officials have usually discouraged African-Americans from seeking dual citizenship on the false excuse that African governments are opposed to it. African governments which have not already done so are, as a matter of urgency, to work out the necessary protocols

to accord dual citizenship to Blacks from the Diaspora. As Marcus Garvey said, it is "Africa for the Africans, at home and abroad."

3. The Black Diaspora constitutes a large reservoir of talent and skilled manpower waiting to be tapped and put to use in developing the Motherland. African countries are to take advantage of this Black reservoir instead of their usual recourse to Whites most of whom are sympathetic to our progress.

4. For their part, Blacks in the Diaspora are to organize a massive "invasion" of the continent by experts of all sorts—teachers, doctors, nurses, engineers, technicians, manufacturers, farmers, entrepreneurs, etc. An "invasion" larger and more sophisticated than the Peace Corps, a fresh revitalized and vastly expanded Operation Crossroads Africa. They should not wait to be invited.

5. The OAU to evolve a continental citizenship scheme to guarantee the possession of a Black Passport as both a right and a privilege.

6. All Blacks are owed by the colonial powers for colonialism, neocolonialism, slavery and the death of millions of Blacks and the physical and mental anguish suffered in the process. Since African free labor built the wealth of the developed world, one half of the gross wealth of the colonial powers is to be transferred by them to the Black world in compensation for general and special damages for the wrongs done to African people.

7. In the USA and Caribbean, reparation for African descendants is to take the form of monetary payment to each individual, who is free to decide to relocate to Africa with the money. Ten percent of individual entitlement is to be put into a United Black Fund (UBF) in the USA, or the Caribbean African Fund (CAF). UBF and CAF are to be managed each by a board representing the youth, women, professional businesspersons, religious leaders,

community leaders, etc. Both trade and development programs.

8. The Pan-African Movement recognizes the effort and energies of individuals and organizations laboring on the issues of reparations on behalf of African people worldwide and encourages those operating from the USA and other countries in the Diaspora to coordinate their efforts with African nations who are also fighting debt slavery created by such institutions as the IMF and the World Bank.

9. Black legislators to fight jointly through their parliaments for our compensation. Reparations to be forced to the top of the political agendas, nationally and internationally.

10. OAU to champion the campaign for full reparations, globally through the UN General Assembly, the UN Security Council, the World Court and direct negotiations with Arab and Western enslavers and colonizers.

11. Compensation received universally, on behalf of Africa, to go into funding aspects of the Black world's Pan-African Development Plan.

12. Black world media to mount continuous publicity and pressure to draw attention to our reparations demands.

13. The Pan-African Movement to assist all reparations efforts around the world and to design appropriate sanctions to be applied against insensitive White and Arab powers in the form of mass withdrawal of services, as and when necessary, to provoke compliance.

Other issues pertinent to nation-building on the Pan-African level were included on the Black Agenda at this inaugural meeting. Acknowledgement is given to the Black Think Tank for the publication of these two items, repatriation and dual citizenship and reparations, on its agenda.

INDEX

A

Abbess. *See* 80,81
Abd al Aziz. *See* 52
Abderrhman Sufi. *See* 70
Abdul Hasson. *See* 69
Abdurrahman ibn Abdullah. *See* 53
Abolition Act. *See* 213
Abolition of Slavery. *See* 213,
215-217,231
ab-Samh ibn Malik. *See* 53
Adams, John. *See* 141
Adoptianists. *See* 34
Africa. *See* 5,7,9,11-19,22,23,26-28,
31,36,43,45-47,49-52,55,62-65,67-69,
72-74,76-78,82,89-92,101-103,107,111;
 See also 119,153,164,167,171,173-176,
189,201,202,207-209,220,224,227,228,
230,233,236,237
  underdeveloped. *See also* 15,16
  underdevelopment of. *See also* 201
Africana curriculum. *See* 22,29
African Americans. *See* 17,22
Africana studies. *See* 22-24,26-29
African Berbers. *See* 65
African Bushmen. *See* 13
African gods. *See* 103
African Gods. *See* 103
African history. *See* 7,28,167
African maroon societies. *See* 169,173
African Moors. *See* 57,60,66,73
Africans. *See* 6,8-10,12-20,22,25,27,29,
31,32,45-47,49,51,57,60,69,73,75,77,80,
82,85,89,90,94,103,110,111,114-116;
 See also 133,138,152,155,165-167,169,
171-177,179,181,183-188,190,192-194,
198-202,204,207-210,213;
 See also 214,216,217,220-222,224,225,
227-230,232,236
African scholars. *See* 9-11,13

African slaves. *See* 82,90,173,175
  treatment of. *See also* 74,167
African Slave Trade. *See* 13,82,111
Africanus, Leo. *See* 43,78,79
  History and Description of Africa,
  The. *See also* 78
African women. *See* 89,94,103,
105-107,109,110,121,224
  in Early Europe. *See also* 4,87,89
Afro-Iberian Moors. *See* 66,224
Alard, Delphin. *See* 125
Alfama. *See* 51
Algeciras. *See* 47
al-Hurr ibn Abdurrahman. *See* 52,53
Almoravids. *See* 90
Ambrosian Mass. *See* 35
American Hussars. *See* 132
American Revolution.
See 141,148,149,151-153,155
  Black regiments in. *See also* 158
  Blacks and mulattos. *See also* 149
Amo, Anthony William. *See* 8
An Absence of Ruins. *See* 26
Anastasius. *See* 38
ancient Greece. *See* 20,102
Angelo, Domenico. *See* 121,130
Angelo, Henry. *See* 121,130
Anonyme, L'Amant. *See* 128,129
Another Life. *See* 25,30
Anthropology. *See* 13
Apollo. *See* 103
Apostolic. *See* 38
Arabs. *See* 43,45,46,65
Arawaks. *See* 19,29
Arbeau. *See* 59
Aristotle. *See* 64
Army of Maxentius, The. *See* 36
Arnould, Sophie. *See* 126
Artemis. *See* 4,104,105

D

United States. *See* 16,17,28,147,166, 221-223,227,230,232

V

Valentia, Viscount. *See* 62

Van Couwenbergh, Christian. *See* 109
  works
    Rape of the negro woman, The
    See also 109

Vandals. *See* 55

Van Sertima, Dr. Ivan. *See* 6,10

Venus of Willendorf. *See* 93

Verlinden, Professor. *See* 90

Vetch, Samuel. *See* 145

Vincente, Gil. *See* 73

W

Walcott, Derek. *See* 25

Warwick, Dionne. *See* 224

Washington, General. *See* 155,157,177

Waterman, William. *See* 77
  works
    The Fardle of Factions.
    See also 77,78

Webster, John. *See* 79

western civilization. *See* 23,24,173,175

West Indies. *See* 24,29,111,141,142,1 44,145,147-151,153,206,218,231,233

Whipple, Prince. *See* 155,161

Whipple, William. *See* 155

White Supremacy. *See* 10,20,223

Whitfield, Charles. *See* 118

Wilberforce, William. *See* 215

Will, George F.. *See* 20

William II of France. *See* 106

Williams, Dr. Chancellor. *See* 30,45

Williams, Dr. Eric. *See* 142,205,206, 214,225

Williams, Francis. *See* 8

William the Conqueror. *See* 59

Wolf, Eric. *See* 25

World War II. *See* 221-223

Y

Yahya ibn Salmah. *See* 53

Yeboah, Samuel Kennedy. *See* 71

Z

Zeus. *See* 103

Zumbi. *See* 1,171,172